low-fat vegetarian
mediterranean
recipes

low-fat vegetarian
mediterranean
recipes

75 delicious meat-free dishes inspired by the sunny food of Greece, France, Spain and Italy, shown step-by-step in 280 stunning photographs

Anne Sheasby

southwater

This edition is published by Southwater
Southwater is an imprint of Anness Publishing Ltd
Hermes House, 88–89 Blackfriars Road, London SE1 8HA
tel. 020 7401 2077; fax 020 7633 9499
www.southwaterbooks.com; www.annesspublishing.com

If you like the images in this book and would like to investigate using them
for publishing, promotions or advertising, please visit our website
www.practicalpictures.com for more information.

© Anness Publishing Ltd 2006

UK agent: The Manning Partnership Ltd
6 The Old Dairy, Melcombe Road, Bath BA2 3LR
tel. 01225 478444; fax 01225 478440
sales@manning-partnership.co.uk

UK distributor: Grantham Book Services Ltd
Isaac Newton Way, Alma Park Industrial Estate, Grantham,
Lincs NG31 9SD; tel. 01476 541080; fax 01476 541061
orders@gbs.tbs-ltd.co.uk

North American agent/distributor: National Book Network
4501 Forbes Boulevard, Suite 200, Lanham, MD 20706
tel. 301 459 3366; fax 301 429 5746; www.nbnbooks.com

Australian agent/distributor: Pan Macmillan Australia
Level 18, St Martins Tower, 31 Market St, Sydney, NSW 2000
tel. 1300 135 113; fax 1300 135 103
customer.service@macmillan.com.au

New Zealand agent/distributor: David Bateman Ltd
30 Tarndale Grove, Off Bush Road, Albany, Auckland
tel. (09) 415 7664; fax (09) 415 8892

Publisher: Joanna Lorenz
Editorial Director: Helen Sudell
Editor: Simona Hill
Designer: Ian Sandom
Cover Designer: Balley Design Associates
Production Controller: Pedro Nelson

Previously published as part of a larger volume,
Low-fat No-fat Mediterranean

Front cover shows Vegetable Moussaka – for recipe, see page 66

10 9 8 7 6 5 4 3 2 1

ACKNOWLEDGEMENTS

Recipes: Pepita Aris, Catherine Atkinson, Mary Banks, Alex Barker, Ghillie
Basan, Judy Bastyra, Angela Boggiano, Jacqueline Clark, Maxine Clark,
Trish Davies, Roz Denny, Joanna Farrow, Jennie Fleetwood, Brian Glover,
Nicola Graimes, Carole Handslip, Christine Ingram, Becky Johnson, Lucy
Knox, Sally Mansfield, Christine McFadden, Jane Milton, Sallie Morris, Rena
Salaman, Jenni Shapter, Marlena Spieler, Liz Trigg, Jenny White, Kate
Whiteman, Lucy Whiteman, Jeni Wright.

Home economists: Eliza Baird, Alex Barker, Caroline Barty, Joanna Farrow,
Annabel Ford, Christine France, Carole Handslip, Kate Jay, Becky Johnson,
Jill Jones, Bridget Sargeson, Jennie Shapter, Carol Tennant, Sunil Vijayakar,
Jenny White.

Photographers: Frank Adam, Tim Auty, Martin Brigdale, Louisa Dare, Nicki
Dowey, Gus Filgate, Ian Garlick, Michelle Garrett, John Heseltine, Amanda
Heywood, Janine Hosegood, Dave Jordan, Dave King, William Lingwood,
Thomas Odulate, Craig Roberson, Simon Smith, Sam Stowell.

NOTES

Bracketed terms are intended for American readers.

For all recipes, quantities are given in both metric and imperial measures
and, where appropriate, in standard cups and spoons. Follow one set, but
not a mixture, because they are not interchangeable.

Standard spoon and cup measures are level. 1 tsp = 5ml,
1 tbsp = 15ml, 1 cup = 250ml/8fl oz.

Australian standard tablespoons are 20ml. Australian readers should use
3 tsp in place of 1 tbsp for measuring small quantities of flour, salt, etc.

American pints are 16fl oz/2 cups. American readers should use
20fl oz/2.5 cups in place of 1 pint when measuring liquids.

Electric oven temperatures in this book are for conventional ovens. When
using a fan oven, the temperature will probably need to be reduced by about
10–20°C/20–40°F. Since ovens vary, you should check with your
manufacturer's instruction book for guidance.

The nutritional analysis given for each recipe is calculated per portion
(i.e. serving or item), unless otherwise stated. If the recipe gives a range,
such as Serves 4–6, then the nutritional analysis will be for the smaller
portion size, i.e. 6 servings. Measurements for sodium do not include salt
added to taste.

Each recipe title in this book is followed by a symbol that indicates
the following:
★ = 5g of fat or less per serving
★★ = 10g of fat or less per serving
★★★ = 15g of fat or less per serving
Medium (US large) eggs are used unless otherwise stated.

CONTENTS

INTRODUCTION

For many of us the Mediterranean conjures up idyllic images of sun-soaked beaches, pretty provincial villages tucked away up in the mountains and on the coast, and sun-drenched olive groves. With it goes the colourful chaos of a bustling food market full of an array of fresh fruit, vegetables, herbs and spices, eating *al fresco* and enjoying the delicious food and drink from the many different regions. This all contributes to an appealing and relaxed vision of life, far away from the hassles of big towns and cities.

Throughout the Mediterranean there is a passion for food and cooking, and eating plays an important part in everyday lives. The warm Mediterranean sea borders a large and varied area and encompasses many different countries, including Spain, southern France, Italy, Greece, Turkey and the Middle East, plus North African countries such as Morocco and Tunisia, as well as the islands of Malta and Cyprus. Much of the fresh produce eaten in Mediterranean countries is grown or produced locally, and quality and freshness of foods is of great importance in these regions. Many of the provincial and regional specialities are created from the seasonal food to hand.

A HEALTHY DIET

Generally speaking, people from the Mediterranean countries live longer and have a lower incidence of cancers, heart disease and obesity than people from countries such as the UK, Canada and the USA – and their diet is probably one of the main reasons why. The types of food traditionally eaten in Mediterranean countries have been proven to offer a variety of health benefits and protection against disease.

The Mediterranean diet generally includes lots of fresh and flavourful sun-ripened fruit and vegetables, fresh herbs, pasta, rice and bread. Although some dishes are high in calories and fat, many traditional dishes from all over the region can still be enjoyed as part of a healthy low-fat eating plan. With a few basic guidelines, therefore, a low-fat Mediterranean diet is simple and easy to achieve – especially when avoiding meat and fish, which are often to blame for the high fat content of dishes.

LOOKING AT FAT

Olive oil is the primary fat used for cooking throughout the Mediterranean. Olive oil is a "healthier" type of fat than that found in dairy products, as it is high in monounsaturated fat and low in saturated fat, and so long as it is used in moderation, it can also be enjoyed as part of a low-fat diet.

Some other ingredients typically used in Mediterranean countries, such as cheeses like Parmesan and mozzarella, are high in fat but are easily substituted with lower-fat options such as reduced-fat mozzarella. Alternatively, in many recipes the quantity of the high-fat food can simply be reduced to lower the fat content of the dish. For many of these dishes, you will be surprised at how little olive oil you will need for cooking some foods, such as sautéed vegetables. Foods such as pasta, beans and rice are also ideal for a low-fat diet as they are naturally high in carbohydrates and low in fat.

Left: Minimal and flavourful ingredients are the hallmark of Mediterranean-style dining.

Above: Pasta is a key ingredient in vegetarian cooking. It is naturally low in fat and the basis of a healthy meal.

Most of us eat fats in some form or another every day and we all need a small amount of fat in our diet to maintain a healthy, balanced eating plan. However, many of us eat far too much fat and we should all be looking to reduce our overall fat intake, especially saturated fats. Regular exercise is also an important factor in a healthy lifestyle.

By making a few simple changes to your diet, you will find it is surprisingly easy to cut down the amount of fat you eat, and you are likely to feel less bloated and more comfortable in your skin, without really noticing any difference to the food you eat.

This book aims to bring you a wide selection of delicious and nutritious dishes from many regions of the Mediterranean, all of which are low in fat, and are ideal to include as part of a healthy vegetarian eating plan.

It includes lots of useful and informative advice. A short introduction provides helpful hints and tips on low-fat and fat-free ingredients and low-fat or fat-free cooking techniques, and practical tips on how to reduce fat and

saturated fat in your diet. This is followed by a collection of 75 delicious and easy-to-follow low-fat Mediterranean recipes for all the family to enjoy. The tempting selection of vegetarian recipes ranges from appetizers, soups and salads, to satisfying main courses, and also includes a tasty collection of home-baked bread and desserts.

THE RECIPES IN THIS BOOK

Each recipe includes a nutritional breakdown, providing at-a-glance calorie and fat contents (including saturated fat content) per serving, as well as other key nutrients such as protein, carbohydrate, calcium, cholesterol, fibre and sodium. All the recipes in this cookbook are low in fat – many containing five grams of fat or less per serving, and a few containing less than one gram of fat per serving.

In the first two chapters of this book – Soups and Appetizers, and Salads and Side Dishes – each recipe contains five grams of fat or less per serving. In the remaining two chapters of the book, which contain recipes for the main course of a meal, and desserts, as well as breads, which can either accompany a meal – in Mediterranean tradition – or form

Above: Herbs and natural sweeteners, such as honey, are a traditional feature of Mediterranean cooking.

the basis of a snack or sandwich, most recipes contain ten grams of fat or less per serving. A few recipes in these chapters, such as Vegetable Moussaka or Spinach with Beans, Raisins and Pine Nuts, contain a slightly higher quantity, 15 grams of fat or less per serving, but are included because they are such classic dishes of the region. For ease of reference, throughout the recipe section, all recipes with a single ★ following the title contain five grams of fat or less, those with ★★ contain ten grams of fat or less and those with ★★★ contain 15 grams of fat or less. All the recipes contain less fat than similar traditional recipes and yet they are still packed full of delicious flavour.

This practical cookbook will enable you to enjoy vegetarian Mediterranean food that is healthy, delicious and nutritious as well as being low in fat.

Left: Olives are an everyday healthy food served throughout the Mediterranean as appetizers or tapas, or cooked in a wide variety of dishes. They contain beneficial fats, but should be eaten in small quantities when following a low-fat diet.

PLANNING A LOW-FAT DIET

Most of us eat about 115g/4oz of fat every day. Yet just 10g/¼oz, about the amount in a single packet of crisps (US potato chips) or a thin slice of Cheddar cheese, is all we actually need.

Current nutritional advice isn't quite that strict though and suggests that we should limit our daily intake of fat to no more than 30 per cent of total calories. Since each gram of fat provides nine calories, this means that for an average intake of 2,000 calories a day, the total daily intake should be around 600 calories or fewer.

CUTTING DOWN ON FAT IN THE DIET

There are lots of simple no-fuss ways of reducing the fat in your diet. Just follow the simple "eat less, try instead" suggestions below to discover how easy it is.

• Eat less butter, margarine, other spreading fats and cooking oils.

• Eat fewer full-fat dairy products such as whole milk, cream, butter, crème fraîche, whole-milk yogurts and hard cheese.

• Try instead semi-skimmed (low-fat) or skimmed milk, low-fat or reduced-fat milk products, low-fat yogurts, low-fat fromage frais and low-fat soft cheeses, reduced-fat hard cheeses such as Cheddar, and reduced-fat crème fraîche.

Above, clockwise from left: Extra virgin olive oil, sunflower oil, safflower oil.

• Try instead reduced-fat spreads, low-fat spreads or fat-free spreads. If you must use butter, make sure it is softened at room temperature and spread it very thinly, or try low-fat cream cheese or low-fat soft cheese for sandwiches and toast.

Buy fresh vegetables and eat them within a few days, as storing them for long periods of time reduces the nutrient levels and the taste.

• Try using low-fat protein products such as peas, beans, lentils or tofu instead of cheese or eggs in recipes.

• Eat fewer hard cooking fats, such as hard margarine.

• Try instead polyunsaturated or monounsaturated oils, such as sunflower, corn or olive oil for cooking (but don't use too much).

• Eat fewer rich salad dressings, and less full-fat mayonnaise.

• Try instead reduced-fat or fat-free mayonnaise or dressings. Make your own salad dressings at home with low-fat yogurt or fromage frais.

• Eat less fried food.

• Try instead fat-free cooking methods such as grilling (broiling), baking, microwaving or steaming whenever possible. Try cooking in non-stick pans with only a very small amount of oil.

• Eat fewer deep-fried and sautéed potatoes.

• Try instead low-fat starchy foods such as pasta, couscous and rice. Choose baked or boiled potatoes.

• Try instead to cook with little or no fat. Use heavy, good quality non-stick pans so that the food doesn't stick. Try using a small amount of spray oil in cooking to control exactly how much fat you are using. Use fat-free or low-fat ingredients for cooking, such as fruit juice, vegetable stock, wine or even beer.

• Eat fewer high-fat snacks, such as chips (French fries), fried snacks and pastries, cakes, doughnuts and cookies.

• Try instead low-fat and fat-free fresh or dried fruits, breadsticks or vegetables. Make your own home-baked low-fat cakes. Buy low-fat and reduced-fat versions of cookies.

Left: Black beans, black-eyed beans (peas) and borlotti beans are valuable sources of protein.

FAT-FREE COOKING METHODS

Once you get into the habit, it's easy to cook without fat. For example, whenever possible grill (broil), bake, microwave and steam foods without the addition of fat, or try stir-frying with little or no fat. Alternatively, try using vegetable stock, wine or fruit juice for cooking, instead of fat.

• By choosing good quality, non-stick cookware, you'll find that the amount of fat needed for cooking foods can be kept to an absolute minimum. If you do need a little fat for cooking, choose an oil that is high in unsaturates, such as olive, sunflower or corn oil, and always use as little as possible, or use an unsaturated spray oil.

• When baking low-fat cakes and cookies, use good quality non-stick bakeware that doesn't need greasing before use, or use baking parchment and only lightly grease before lining.
• Look for non-stick coated fabric sheets. This re-usable non-stick material is amazingly versatile, as it can be cut to size and used to line cake tins (pans), baking sheets or frying pans. Heat-resistant up to 550°F and microwave-safe, it will last for up to five years.
• Sauté vegetables in vegetable stock, wine or fruit juice instead of oil.
• Try a yogurt or just vinegar or lemon juice for salad dressings.

• When grilling (broiling) foods, the addition of fat is often unnecessary. If the food shows signs of drying, lightly brush with a small amount of unsaturated oil, such as olive, sunflower or corn oil.
• Microwaved foods rarely need the addition of fat, so add herbs or spices for extra flavour and colour.

• Steaming and boiling are easy, fat-free ways of cooking many foods. When boiling vegetables, use just a little water and save the stock produced for use in another recipe.
• Try braising vegetables in the oven in vegetable stock, wine or simply water with the addition of some chopped fresh or dried herbs.

• Don't pan-fry vegetables, such as onions, mushrooms, carrots and celery, in oil or butter. Instead, put the sliced vegetables into a non-stick pan with about 150ml/¼ pint/⅔ cup vegetable stock. Cover and cook for 5 minutes or until the vegetables are tender and the stock has reduced.
• Parcel cooking vegetables and fruit allows the food to cook in its own juices and the steam created, holding in all the flavour and nutrient value and eliminating the need for oil or fats. Enclose food in indvidual foil or paper parcels, add extra flavourings such as wine, herbs and spices, if you like, twist or fold parcel ends to secure and ensure juices can't run out, then either bake, steam or cook on a barbecue.

• When serving vegetables resist the temptation to add butter or margarine. Instead, sprinkle with chopped fresh herbs or ground spices.

LOW-FAT SPREADS IN COOKING

There is a huge variety of low-fat and reduced-fat spreads available at our supermarkets, along with some spreads that are very low in fat. Generally speaking, any very low-fat spreads with a fat content of around 20 per cent or less have a high water content. These are unsuitable for cooking and can only be used for spreading.

Fat and Calorie Contents of Food

The figures show the weight of fat in grams and the energy content per 100g (3½oz) of each of the following foods used in Mediterranean cooking. Use the table to help work out the fat content of favourite dishes.

	Fat (g)	Energy		Fat (g)	Energy
VEGETABLES			Dried mixed fruit	0.4	268kcals/1114kJ
Asparagus	0	15kcals/63kJ	Figs	0	43kcals/185kJ
Aubergines (eggplants)	0.4	15kcals/63kJ	Grapefruit	0.1	30kcals/126kJ
Beetroot (beets), cooked	0.1	36kcals/151kJ	Grapes	0	63kcals/265kJ
(Bell) peppers	0.4	32kcals/128kJ	Lemons, with peel	0.2	9kcals/38kJ
Broad (fava) beans	0.8	48kcals/204kJ	Melon	0	32kcals/135kJ
Broccoli	0.9	33kcals/138kJ	Olives, green	11	112kcals/422kJ
Cabbage	0.4	26kcals/109kJ	Oranges	0.1	37kcals/158kJ
Carrots	0.3	35kcals/146kJ	Peaches/nectarines	0.1	33kcals/142kJ
Cauliflower	0.9	34kcals/146kJ	Pears	0.1	40kcals/169kJ
Celery, raw	0.2	33kcals/142kJ	Pomegranate	0.2	51kcals/218kJ
Courgettes (zucchini)	0.4	18kcals/74kJ	Almonds	55.8	612kcals/2534kJ
Cucumber	0.1	10kcals/40kJ	Brazil nuts	68.2	682kcals/2813kJ
Fennel	0	14kcals/56kJ	Hazelnuts	63.5	650kcals/2685kJ
Globe artichoke	0	9kcals/35kJ	Peanut butter, smooth	53.7	623kcal/2581kJ
Green beans	0	22kcals/92kJ	Pine nuts	68.6	688kcals/2840kJ
Jerusalem artichoke	0	41kcals/207kJ	Pistachio nuts	58.3	632kcals/2650kJ
Mushrooms	0.5	13kcals/55kJ	Walnuts	68.5	688kcals/2840kJ
Okra	0	26kcals/110kJ			
Onions	0.2	36kcals/151kJ	**BEANS, PULSES AND CEREALS**		
Peas	1.5	83kcals/344kJ	Black-eyed beans (peas), cooked	1.8	116kcals/494kJ
Potatoes	0.2	75kcals/318kJ	Brown rice, raw	2.8	357kcals/1518kJ
Chips (French fries), home-made	6.7	189kcals/796kJ	Bulgur wheat	2.5	319kcals/1340kJ
Chips, retail	12.4	162kcals/1924kJ	Butter beans, canned	0.5	77kcals/327kJ
Oven-chips, frozen baked	4.2	162kcals/687kJ	Chickpeas, canned	2.9	115kcals/487kJ
Potato crisps (US potato chips)	34.2	530kcals/1924kJ	Couscous, cooked	0	112kcals/470kJ
Spinach, fresh, cooked	0	21kcals/84kJ	Hummus	12.6	187kcals/781kJ
Tomatoes	0.3	17kcals/73kJ	Pasta, white, raw	1.8	342kcals/1456kJ
			Pasta, wholemeal		
FRUITS AND NUTS			(whole-wheat), uncooked	2.5	324kcals/1379kJ
Apples, eating	0.1	47kcals/199kJ	Polenta	1.6	330kcals/1383kJ
Avocados	19.5	190kcals/784kJ	Red kidney beans, canned	0.6	100kcals/424kJ
Bananas	0.3	95kcals/403kJ	Red lentils, cooked	0.4	100kcals/424kJ
Dates	0	226/kcals/970kJ	White rice, raw	3.6	383kcals/1630kJ

Below: Vegetables are very low in fat. Eat them raw for a filling snack, or steam them to retain maximum nutritional value.

Below: Cheese is very high in fat and should be eaten as an occasional treat when following a low-fat diet.

Above: Vegetables contain plenty of dietary fibre and are valuable sources especially of vitamins A, C and E.

	Fat (g)	Energy
BAKING AND SWEET SPREADS		
Bread, brown	2.0	218kcals/927kJ
Bread, white	1.9	235kcals/1002kJ
Bread, wholemeal (whole-wheat)	2.5	215kcaqls/914kJ
Chocolate, milk	30.7	520kcals/2157kJ
Chocolate, plain (semisweet)	28.0	510kcals/2116kJ
Croissants	20.3	360kcals/1505kJ
Digestive biscuits (graham crackers)	20.9	471kcals/1978kJ
Reduced-fat digestive biscuits	16.4	467kcals/1965kJ
Fatless sponge cake	6.1	294kcals/1245kJ
Flapjacks	26.6	484kcals/2028kJ
Flour, plain (all-purpose) white	1.3	341kcals/1450kJ
Flour, self-raising (self-rising)	1.2	330kcals/1407kJ
Flour, wholemeal (whole-wheat)	2.2	310kcals/1318kJ
Honey	0	288kcals/1229kJ
Jam	0.26	268kcals/1114kJ
Madeira cake	16.9	393kcals/1652kJ
Shortbread	26.1	498kcals/2087kJ
Sugar, white	0.3	94kcals/1680kJ
FATS, OILS AND EGGS		
Butter	81.7	737kcals/3031kJ
Margarine	81.6	739kcals/3039kJ
Low-fat spread	40.5	390kcals/1605kJ
Very low-fat spread	25.0	273kcals/1128kJ
Cooking oil	99.9	899kcals/3696kJ
Corn oil	99.9	899kcals/3696kJ
Olive oil	99.9	899kcals/3696kJ
Safflower oil	99.9	899kcals/3696kJ
Eggs	10.8	147kcals/612kJ
Egg yolk	30.5	399kcals/1402kJ
Egg white	Trace	36kcals/153kJ
French dressing	49.4	462kcals/1902kJ
Fat-free dressing	1.2	67kcals/282kJ
Mayonnaise	75.6	691kcals/2843kJ
Mayonnaise, reduced calorie	28.1	288kcals/1188kJ

Above: Eating a variety of different fruits and vegetables every day is essential to good health.

	Fat (g)	Energy
CREAM, MILK AND CHEESE		
Cream, double (heavy)	48.0	449kcals/1849kJ
Reduced-fat double (heavy) cream	24.0	243kcals/1002kJ
Cream, single (light)	19.1	198kcals/817kJ
Cream, whipping	39.3	373kcals/1539kJ
Crème fraîche	40.0	379kcals/156kJ
Reduced-fat crème fraîche	15.0	165kcals/683kJ
Milk, skimmed	0.1	33kcals/130kJ
Milk, full cream (whole)	3.9	66kcals/275kJ
Brie	26.9	319kcals/1323kJ
Cheddar cheese	34.4	412kcals/1708kJ
Cheddar-type, reduced-fat	15.0	261kcals/1091kJ
Cottage cheese	3.9	98kcals/413kJ
Cream cheese	47.4	439kcals/1807kJ
Curd cheese (medium-fat)	11.7	173kcals/723kJ
Edam cheese	25.4	333kcals/1382kJ
Feta cheese	20.2	250kcals/1037kJ
Fromage frais, plain	7.1	113kcals/469kJ
Fromage frais, very low-fat	0.2	58kcals/247kJ
Mozzarella cheese	21.0	289kcals/1204kJ
Parmesan cheese	32.7	452kcals/1880kJ
Ricotta cheese	10	150kcals/625kJ
Skimmed-milk soft cheese	trace	74kcals/313kJ
Low-fat yogurt, natural (plain)	0.8	56kcals/236kJ
Greek (US strained plain) yogurt	9.1	115kcals/477kJ
Reduced-fat Greek yogurt	5.0	80kcals/335kJ

SOUPS AND APPETIZERS

You will find a tempting collection of light and tasty soups and appetizers from different regions of the Mediterranean in this chapter, all are full of flavour yet low in fat. The recipes featured here include classics such as Spanish Potato and Garlic Soup, Ribollita, Spiced Dolmades and Tsatziki.

ROASTED GARLIC AND BUTTERNUT SQUASH SOUP WITH TOMATO SALSA ★

THIS IS A WONDERFUL, RICHLY FLAVOURED SOUP. A SPOONFUL OF THE HOT AND SPICY TOMATO SALSA GIVES BITE TO THE SWEET TASTE OF THE SQUASH AND GARLIC.

SERVES SIX

INGREDIENTS

2 garlic bulbs, outer papery
  skin removed
a few fresh thyme sprigs
15ml/1 tbsp olive oil
1 large butternut squash, halved
  and seeded
2 onions, chopped
5ml/1 tsp ground coriander
1.2 litres/2 pints/5 cups vegetable or
  chicken stock
30–45ml/2–3 tbsp chopped fresh
  oregano or marjoram
salt and ground black pepper
For the salsa
4 large ripe tomatoes, halved
  and seeded
1 red (bell) pepper, seeded
1 large fresh red chilli, halved
  and seeded
15ml/1 tbsp extra virgin olive oil
15ml/1 tbsp balsamic vinegar
pinch of caster (superfine) sugar

1 Preheat the oven to 220°C/425°F/
Gas 7. Place the garlic bulbs on a piece
of foil, add the thyme and drizzle over
7.5ml/1½ tsp of the oil, then fold the foil
around the garlic bulbs to enclose them.

2 Transfer the foil parcel to a baking sheet
with the butternut squash and lightly
brush the squash with 10ml/2 tsp of the
remaining olive oil. Place the tomatoes,
red pepper and fresh chilli for the salsa
on the baking sheet.

3 Roast the vegetables for 25 minutes,
then remove the tomatoes, pepper and
chilli. Reduce the oven temperature to
190°C/375°F/Gas 5 and roast the squash
and garlic for a further 20–25 minutes,
or until the squash is tender.

4 Heat the remaining oil in a large,
heavy non-stick pan and cook the
onions and ground coriander gently for
about 10 minutes, or until softened and
just beginning to brown.

5 Meanwhile, skin the pepper and
chilli, then process them in a blender or
food processor with the tomatoes and
the olive oil for the salsa. Stir in the
balsamic vinegar and seasoning to
taste, adding a pinch of caster sugar,
if necessary, to moderate the taste.

6 Squeeze the roasted garlic out of its
papery skin into the onions and scoop
the squash out of its skin, adding it
to the pan too. Add the stock, 5ml/1 tsp
salt and plenty of black pepper. Bring to
the boil, then simmer for 10 minutes.

7 Stir in half the chopped oregano or
marjoram and cool the soup slightly
before processing it in a blender or food
processor. Alternatively, use a wooden
spoon to press the soup through a fine
sieve (strainer) placed over a bowl.

8 Reheat the soup without allowing it
to boil, then taste for seasoning before
ladling it into warmed bowls. Top each
with a spoonful of salsa and sprinkle with
the remaining chopped oregano or
marjoram. Serve immediately.

Energy 120kcal/502kJ; Protein 5g; Carbohydrate 15.7g, of which sugars 9.1g; Fat 4.6g, of which saturates 0.8g, of which polyunsaturates 0.6g; Cholesterol 0mg; Calcium 70mg; Fibre 4.6g; Sodium 10mg.

PLUM TOMATO AND FRESH BASIL SOUP ★

A DELICIOUS SOUP FOR LATE SUMMER WHEN FRESH TOMATOES ARE AT THEIR RIPEST AND MOST FLAVOURSOME. SERVE WITH CRUSTY FRESH ITALIAN OR FRENCH BREAD, OR WARM SODA BREAD.

SERVES SIX

INGREDIENTS
    15ml/1 tbsp olive oil
    1 onion, finely chopped
    900g/2lb ripe plum tomatoes, chopped
    1 garlic clove, chopped
    about 750ml/1¼ pints/3 cups
      vegetable stock
    120ml/4fl oz/½ cup dry white wine
    30ml/2 tbsp sun-dried tomato
      purée (paste)
    30ml/2 tbsp shredded fresh basil
    60ml/4 tbsp single (light) cream
    salt and ground black pepper
    fresh basil leaves, to garnish

VARIATION
This soup can also be served chilled. Pour into a container after straining, allow to cool to room temperature and then chill in the refrigerator for 4 hours.

1 Heat the oil in a large pan until hot. Add the onion and cook gently for about 5 minutes, stirring frequently, until softened but not brown.

2 Stir in the tomatoes and garlic, and add the stock, wine and sun-dried tomato purée. Season to taste. Bring to the boil, then reduce the heat, partially cover the pan and simmer gently for 20 minutes, stirring occasionally to stop the tomatoes sticking to the pan base.

3 Process the soup with the shredded basil in a blender or food processor, then press through a sieve (strainer) into a clean pan.

4 Add the cream and heat through gently without boiling, stirring. Check the consistency and add a little more stock or water if necessary, then taste for seasoning. Pour into warmed bowls and garnish with basil leaves. Serve immediately.

Energy 81kcal/338kJ; Protein 1.7g; Carbohydrate 6.1g, of which sugars 5.9g; Fat 4.2g, of which saturates 1.6g, of which polyunsaturates 0.5g; Cholesterol 6mg; Calcium 25mg; Fibre 1.7g; Sodium 24mg.

CATALAN POTATO AND BROAD BEAN SOUP ★

BROAD BEANS ARE ALSO KNOWN AS FAVA BEANS. WHILE THEY ARE IN SEASON FRESH BEANS ARE PERFECT, BUT CANNED OR FROZEN WILL MAKE AN IDEAL SUBSTITUTE FOR THIS FLAVOURFUL SOUP.

SERVES SIX

INGREDIENTS
   15ml/1 tbsp olive oil
   2 onions, chopped
   3 large floury potatoes, diced
   450g/1lb fresh broad (fava) beans
   1.75 litres/3 pints/7½ cups
      vegetable stock
   1 bunch fresh coriander (cilantro),
      finely chopped
   60ml/4 tbsp single (light) cream
   salt and ground black pepper
   fresh coriander (cilantro) leaves,
      to garnish

COOK'S TIP
Broad beans sometimes have a tough outer skin, particularly if they are large. To remove this, cook the beans briefly, peel off the skin, and add the tender centre part to the soup.

1 Heat the oil in a large pan, add the onions and cook, stirring occasionally, for 5 minutes, until soft but not brown.

2 Add the potatoes, beans (reserving a few for garnishing) and stock to the mixture in the pan and bring to the boil, then simmer for 5 minutes. Stir in the chopped coriander and simmer for a further 10 minutes. Remove the pan from the heat and cool slightly.

3 Process the mixture in batches in a blender or food processor until smooth, then return the soup to the rinsed-out pan.

4 Stir in the cream, season with salt and pepper, and reheat gently without boiling. Serve garnished with coriander leaves and the reserved beans.

Energy 181kcal/765kJ; Protein 8.6g; Carbohydrate 28g, of which sugars 4.6g; Fat 4.7g, of which saturates 1.7g, of which polyunsaturates 0.6g; Cholesterol 6mg; Calcium 82mg; Fibre 6.8g; Sodium 24mg.

SPANISH POTATO AND GARLIC SOUP ★

SERVED IN EARTHENWARE DISHES, THIS CLASSIC SPANISH SOUP REALLY IS ONE TO SAVOUR.

SERVES SIX

INGREDIENTS
   15ml/1 tbsp olive oil
   1 large onion, thinly sliced
   4 garlic cloves, crushed
   1 large potato, halved and cut into
      thin slices
   5ml/1 tsp paprika
   400g/14oz can chopped
      tomatoes, drained
   5ml/1 tsp chopped fresh
      thyme leaves
   900ml/1½ pints/3¾ cups
      vegetable stock
   5ml/1 tsp cornflour (cornstarch)
   salt and ground black pepper
   chopped fresh thyme leaves,
      to garnish

1 Heat the oil in a large pan. Add the onions, garlic, potato and paprika and cook for 5 minutes, or until the onions are softened, but not browned.

2 Add the tomatoes, thyme and stock. Bring to the boil, reduce the heat and simmer for 15–20 minutes until tender.

3 Blend the cornflour with a little water in a small bowl to form a paste, then stir into the soup. Simmer for 5 minutes, stirring, until the soup is thickened.

4 Break the potatoes up slightly. Season to taste. Sprinkle with the chopped thyme leaves to garnish.

Energy 74kcal/313kJ; Protein 1.6g; Carbohydrate 12.8g, of which sugars 4.8g; Fat 2.2g, of which saturates 0.4g, of which polyunsaturates 0.4g; Cholesterol 0mg; Calcium 17mg; Fibre 1.6g; Sodium 12mg.

MEDITERRANEAN FARMHOUSE SOUP ★

ROOT VEGETABLES FORM THE BASE OF THIS FLAVOURFUL, CHUNKY, MINESTRONE-STYLE SOUP.
YOU CAN VARY THE VEGETABLES ACCORDING TO WHAT YOU HAVE TO HAND.

SERVES SIX

INGREDIENTS
15ml/1 tbsp olive oil
1 onion, roughly chopped
3 carrots, cut into large chunks
175–200g/6–7oz turnips, cut into large chunks
about 175g/6oz swede (rutabaga), cut into large chunks
400g/14oz can chopped Italian tomatoes
15ml/1 tbsp tomato purée (paste)
5ml/1 tsp dried mixed herbs
5ml/1 tsp dried oregano
50g/2oz/½ cup dried peppers, washed and thinly sliced (optional)
1.5 litres/2½ pints/6¼ cups vegetable stock or water
50g/2oz/½ cup dried small macaroni or conchiglie
400g/14oz can red kidney beans, rinsed and drained
30ml/2 tbsp chopped fresh flat leaf parsley
salt and ground black pepper
freshly grated Parmesan cheese, to serve (optional)

1 Heat the oil in a large non-stick pan, add the onion and cook over a low heat for about 5 minutes until softened. Add the fresh vegetables, tomatoes, tomato purée, herbs and peppers, if using. Season to taste. Pour in the stock or water and bring to the boil. Stir well, cover, reduce the heat and simmer for 30 minutes, stirring occasionally.

COOK'S TIP
Packets of dried Italian peppers are sold in supermarkets and delicatessens. They are piquant and firm with a "meaty" bite to them, which makes them ideal for adding to vegetarian soups.

2 Add the pasta and bring to the boil, stirring. Reduce the heat and simmer uncovered, stirring frequently, until the pasta is only just *al dente*: about 5 minutes or according to the instructions on the packet.

3 Stir in the beans. Heat through for 2–3 minutes, then remove from the heat and stir in the chopped parsley. Taste the soup for seasoning. Serve hot in warmed soup bowls, with grated Parmesan handed around separately, if you like.

Energy 154kcal/651kJ; Protein 7g; Carbohydrate 26.6g, of which sugars 10.3g; Fat 2.9g, of which saturates 0.4g, of which polyunsaturates 0.7g; Cholesterol 0mg; Calcium 106mg; Fibre 7.2g; Sodium 282mg.

PISTOU ★

A DELICIOUS CHUNKY VEGETABLE SOUP SERVED WITH TOMATO PESTO. SERVE IN SMALL PORTIONS AS AN APPETIZER, OR IN LARGER BOWLS WITH CRUSTY BREAD AS A FILLING LUNCH.

SERVES SIX

INGREDIENTS

1 courgette (zucchini), diced
1 small potato, diced
1 shallot, chopped
1 carrot, diced
400g/14oz can chopped tomatoes
1.2 litres/2 pints/5 cups vegetable
   stock
50g/2oz green beans, cut into
   1cm/½in lengths
50g/2oz/½ cup frozen petits pois
   (baby peas)
50g/2oz/½ cup small pasta shapes
30ml/2 tbsp pesto sauce
10ml/2 tsp tomato purée (paste)
salt and ground black pepper
freshly grated Parmesan or Pecorino
   cheese, to serve (optional)

1 Place the courgette, potato, shallot, carrot and tomatoes in a large pan. Add the vegetable stock and season with salt and plenty of black pepper. Bring to the boil over a medium heat, then reduce the heat, cover the pan and simmer for 20 minutes.

2 Add the green beans and petits pois to the pan and bring the soup back to the boil. Boil the mixture briefly for about a minute.

VARIATIONS
• To strengthen the tomato flavour, try using tomato-flavoured spaghetti, broken into small lengths, instead of the small pasta shapes.
• Sun-dried tomato purée (paste) can be used instead of regular.

3 Add the pasta. Simmer the soup for a further 10 minutes, or until the pasta is tender. Taste and adjust the seasoning.

4 Ladle the soup into bowls. Mix together the pesto and tomato purée; stir a little into each serving. Sprinkle with grated cheese, if you like.

Energy 96kcal/406kJ; Protein 4.1g; Carbohydrate 15g, of which sugars 5.3g; Fat 2.7g, of which saturates 0.7g, of which polyunsaturates 0.5g; Cholesterol 2mg; Calcium 47mg; Fibre 2.5g; Sodium 37mg.

RIBOLLITA ★

THIS SOUP IS RATHER LIKE AN ITALIAN MINESTRONE. IT IS BASED ON TOMATOES, BUT WITH BEANS INSTEAD OF PASTA. IN ITALY IT IS TRADITIONALLY LADLED OVER BREAD AND A GREEN VEGETABLE.

SERVES EIGHT

INGREDIENTS

   350g/12oz well-flavoured tomatoes,
     preferably plum tomatoes
   15ml/1 tbsp extra virgin olive oil or
     sunflower oil
   2 onions, chopped
   2 carrots, sliced
   4 garlic cloves, crushed
   2 celery sticks, thinly sliced
   1 fennel bulb, trimmed and chopped
   2 large courgettes (zucchini),
     thinly sliced
   400g/14oz can chopped tomatoes
   15ml/1 tbsp pesto sauce
   900ml/1½ pints/3¾ cups
     vegetable stock
   400g/14oz can haricot (navy) or
     borlotti beans, drained
   salt and ground black pepper
To finish
   10ml/2 tsp extra virgin olive oil
   450g/1lb fresh young spinach
   8 small slices white bread
   Parmesan or Pecorino cheese
     shavings, to serve (optional)

1 To skin the tomatoes, plunge them into boiling water for 30 seconds, refresh in cold water and then peel off and discard the skins. Chop the tomato flesh and set it aside.

2 Heat the oil in a large non-stick pan. Add the onions, carrots, garlic, celery and fennel and cook gently for 10 minutes. Add the courgettes and cook for a further 2 minutes.

3 Stir in the chopped fresh and canned tomatoes, pesto, stock and beans, and bring to the boil. Reduce the heat, cover the pan and simmer gently for 25–30 minutes, or until the vegetables are completely tender and the stock is full of flavour. Season the soup with salt and pepper to taste.

4 To finish, heat the oil in a non-stick frying pan and cook the spinach for 2 minutes, or until wilted. Place a slice of bread in each serving bowl, top with the spinach and then ladle the soup over the spinach. Serve with a little Parmesan or Pecorino cheese to sprinkle on top, if you like.

Energy 154kcal/648kJ; Protein 7.9g; Carbohydrate 21.3g, of which sugars 8.3g; Fat 4.7g, of which saturates 0.7g, of which polyunsaturates 1g; Cholesterol 0mg; Calcium 156mg; Fibre 6.4g; Sodium 379mg.

PEA SOUP WITH GARLIC ★

IF YOU KEEP PEAS IN THE FREEZER, YOU CAN RUSTLE UP THIS DELICIOUS LOW-FAT SOUP IN MINUTES.
IT HAS A WONDERFULLY SWEET TASTE AND SMOOTH TEXTURE AND IS GREAT SERVED WITH CRUSTY
BREAD AND GARNISHED WITH MINT.

SERVES SIX

INGREDIENTS
15g/½oz/1 tbsp butter
1 garlic clove, crushed
900g/2lb/8 cups frozen peas
1.2 litres/2 pints/5 cups vegetable
  stock
salt and ground black pepper
fresh mint leaves, to garnish

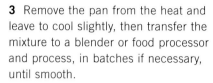

1 Heat the butter in a large non-stick pan and add the garlic. Cook gently for 2–3 minutes, or until softened.

2 Add the peas. Cook for 1–2 minutes, then pour in the stock. Bring to the boil, reduce to a simmer, cover and cook for 5–6 minutes, or until tender.

3 Remove the pan from the heat and leave to cool slightly, then transfer the mixture to a blender or food processor and process, in batches if necessary, until smooth.

4 Return the soup to the rinsed-out pan and heat through gently, stirring. Season to taste with salt and black pepper. Ladle into warmed soup bowls to serve and garnish with mint leaves.

COOK'S TIPS
• When buying fresh garlic, choose plump bulbs with tightly packed cloves and dry skin.
• Avoid any garlic bulbs with soft, shrivelled cloves or green shoots.

Energy 143kcal/593kJ; Protein 10.4g; Carbohydrate 17g, of which sugars 3.5g; Fat 4.3g, of which saturates 1.8g, of which polyunsaturates 1.1g; Cholesterol 5mg; Calcium 32mg; Fibre 7.1g; Sodium 17mg.

TOMATO AND GARLIC BREAD ★

A BASKET OF WARM, CRUSTY, GARLIC-FLAVOURED BREAD IS A COMPULSORY ADDITION TO ANY TAPAS TABLE, ESPECIALLY WHEN IT IS LOW IN FAT TOO!

SERVES SIX

INGREDIENTS

4 large ripe tomatoes,
   roughly chopped
2 garlic cloves, roughly chopped
1.5ml/¼ tsp sea salt
grated rind and juice of ½ lemon
5ml/1 tsp soft light brown sugar
1 flat loaf of bread, such as ciabatta
15ml/1 tbsp olive oil
freshly ground black pepper

3 While the bread is baking, stir the lemon juice and olive oil into the tomato mixture. Cook, uncovered, for a further 8 minutes, or until the mixture is thick and pulpy, stirring occasionally.

4 Spread the tomato mixture on the hot bread pieces, sprinkle with black pepper and serve immediately.

1 Preheat the oven to 200°C/400°F/ Gas 6. Place the tomatoes, garlic, salt, lemon rind and brown sugar in a small pan. Cover and cook gently for 5 minutes, or until the tomatoes have released their juices and the mixture is quite watery.

2 Split the loaf in half horizontally, then cut each half widthways into 3 equal pieces. Place on a baking sheet and bake for 5–8 minutes, or until hot, crisp and golden brown.

Energy 145kcal/613kJ; Protein 4.6g; Carbohydrate 24.1g, of which sugars 4.6g; Fat 4g, of which saturates 0.6g, of which polyunsaturates 0.7g; Cholesterol 0mg; Calcium 54mg; Fibre 1.7g; Sodium 222mg.

MARINATED PIMIENTOS ★

PIMIENTOS ARE SIMPLY SKINNED, COOKED PEPPERS. YOU CAN BUY THEM IN CANS OR JARS, BUT THEY ARE MUCH TASTIER WHEN HOME-MADE. THEY MAKE A DELICIOUS APPETIZER.

SERVES FOUR

INGREDIENTS
    3 red (bell) peppers
    2 small garlic cloves, crushed
    45ml/3 tbsp chopped fresh parsley
    15ml/1 tbsp sherry vinegar
    25ml/1½ tbsp olive oil
    salt, to taste

1 Preheat the grill (broiler) to high. Place the peppers on a baking sheet and grill (broil) for 8–12 minutes, turning occasionally, until the skins have blistered and blackened. Remove the peppers from the heat, cover with a clean dish towel and leave for 5 minutes so that the steam softens the skin.

2 Make a small cut in the bottom of each pepper and squeeze out the juice into a jug. Peel away the skin and cut the peppers in half. Remove and discard the core and seeds.

3 Using a sharp knife, cut each pepper in half lengthways into 1cm/½in-wide strips. Place them in a small bowl.

4 Whisk the garlic, parsley, vinegar and oil into the pepper juices. Add salt to taste. Pour over the pepper strips and toss well. Cover and leave to marinate for 2–4 hours. Serve at room temperature.

Energy 84kcal/349kJ; Protein 1.7g; Carbohydrate 8.7g, of which sugars 8.3g; Fat 4.9g, of which saturates 0.8g, of which polyunsaturates 0.6g; Cholesterol 0mg; Calcium 33mg; Fibre 2.7g; Sodium 9mg.

OVEN-BAKED PEPPERS AND TOMATOES ★

MAKE SURE THERE IS A BASKET OF WARM, FRESH BREAD ON HAND SO THAT NONE OF THE DELICIOUS JUICES FROM THIS LOW-FAT APPETIZER ARE WASTED.

SERVES EIGHT

INGREDIENTS
2 red (bell) peppers
2 yellow (bell) peppers
1 red onion, sliced
2 garlic cloves, halved
6 plum tomatoes, quartered
50g/2oz/⅓ cup black olives
5ml/1 tsp soft light brown sugar
45ml/3 tbsp sherry
3–4 rosemary sprigs
20ml/4 tsp olive oil
salt and ground black pepper

1 Preheat the oven to 200°C/400°F/ Gas 6. Seed the red and yellow peppers, then cut each into 12 even strips.

2 Place the peppers, onion, garlic, tomatoes and olives in a large roasting pan. Sprinkle over the sugar, then pour over the sherry. Season well, cover with foil and bake for 30 minutes.

3 Remove the foil from the tin and stir the vegetables to mix well. Add the rosemary sprigs.

4 Drizzle over the olive oil. Return the pan to the oven for a further 20–30 minutes, or until the vegetables are tender. Serve hot.

Energy 78kcal/327kJ; Protein 1.7g; Carbohydrate 10g, of which sugars 9.3g; Fat 3.1g, of which saturates 0.5g, of which polyunsaturates 0.6g; Cholesterol 0mg; Calcium 21mg; Fibre 2.6g; Sodium 152mg.

AUBERGINE PURÉE ★

SERVE THIS VELVET-TEXTURED LOW-FAT DIP IN THE SUMMERTIME, WHEN THERE IS A READY SUPPLY OF FIRM, GLOSSY AUBERGINES TO MAKE IT WITH, AND CRISP VEGETABLES TO SERVE IT WITH.

SERVES FOUR

INGREDIENTS

1 large aubergine (eggplant)
25ml/1½ tbsp olive oil
2 garlic cloves, finely chopped
30ml/2 tbsp chopped fresh
  coriander (cilantro)
juice of ½ lemon
cayenne pepper, to taste
salt and ground black pepper
fresh coriander (cilantro) leaves,
  to garnish

1 Preheat the oven to 200°C/400°F/ Gas 6. Place the aubergine on a baking sheet and bake for 30 minutes, or until the skin is blackened and the aubergine is very soft.

2 Remove from the oven and allow the aubergine to cool slightly. Cut it in half and use a spoon to scoop out the flesh into a bowl; discard the skin.

COOK'S TIP
The aubergine can be grilled (broiled) for 20 minutes; keep turning it while cooking.

3 Mash the aubergine flesh using a fork to form a purée.

4 Stir in the olive oil, garlic, chopped coriander and lemon juice, with enough cayenne, salt and pepper to suit your taste. Allow the mixture to cool. Serve garnished with coriander leaves.

Energy 57kcal/236kJ; Protein 1.3g; Carbohydrate 2.9g, of which sugars 1.6g; Fat 4.6g, of which saturates 0.7g, of which polyunsaturates 0.5g; Cholesterol 0mg; Calcium 9mg; Fibre 1.8g; Sodium 2mg.

GUACAMOLE <u>WITH</u> CRUDITÉS ★

THIS FRESH-TASTING SPICY DIP IS MADE USING PEAS INSTEAD OF THE TRADITIONAL AVOCADOS. THE PEAS CREATE A DIFFERENT TASTE AND TEXTURE, BUT FOR A LOW-FAT DIP, IT'S WELL WORTH TRYING. SERVE WITH FRUIT AND SALAD VEGETABLES.

SERVES SIX

INGREDIENTS
350g/12oz/3 cups frozen peas, thawed
1 garlic clove, crushed
2 spring onions (scallions), trimmed and chopped
5ml/1 tsp finely grated lime rind
juice of 1 lime
2.5ml/½ tsp ground cumin
dash of Tabasco sauce
15ml/1 tbsp reduced-calorie mayonnaise
30ml/2 tbsp chopped fresh coriander (cilantro)
salt and ground black pepper
pinch of paprika and lime slices, to garnish
For the crudités
6 baby carrots
2 celery sticks
1 red-skinned eating apple
1 pear
15ml/1 tbsp lemon or lime juice
6 baby corn

1 Put the peas, garlic clove, spring onions, lime rind and juice, cumin, Tabasco sauce, mayonnaise and salt and ground black pepper in a blender or food processor and process for a few minutes, or until smooth.

2 Add the coriander and process for a few seconds. Spoon the mixture into a serving bowl, cover with clear film (plastic wrap) and chill for 30 minutes, to let the flavours develop.

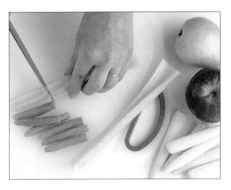

3 For the crudités, trim and peel the carrots. Halve the celery sticks lengthways and trim into sticks the same length as the carrots. Quarter, core and thickly slice the apple and pear, then dip into the lemon or lime juice to prevent discoloration. Arrange with the baby corn on a serving platter.

4 Sprinkle the paprika over the guacamole and garnish with lime slices. Serve.

VARIATION
Use ground coriander in place of ground cumin, if you like.

Energy 93kcal/386kJ; Protein 5.2g; Carbohydrate 14.7g, of which sugars 9g; Fat 1.9g, of which saturates 0.3g, of which polyunsaturates 0.9g; Cholesterol 1mg; Calcium 41mg; Fibre 5.1g; Sodium 232mg.

SPICED DOLMADES ★

THESE TASTY DOLMADES CONTAIN SUMAC, A SPICE WITH A SHARP LEMON FLAVOUR. IT IS AVAILABLE FROM SPECIALIST STORES. SERVE THESE DOLMADES WITH A MIXTURE OF OTHER TRADITIONAL APPETIZERS, SUCH AS OLIVES AND CRUSTY BREAD, FOR A SPECIAL DINNER.

MAKES TWENTY

INGREDIENTS
  20 vacuum-packed vine leaves in brine
  90g/3½oz/½ cup long grain rice
  25ml/1½ tbsp olive oil
  1 small onion, finely chopped
  50g/2oz/½ cup pine nuts
  45ml/3 tbsp raisins
  30ml/2 tbsp chopped fresh mint
  2.5ml/½ tsp ground cinnamon
  2.5ml/½ tsp ground allspice
  10ml/2 tsp ground sumac
  10ml/2 tsp lemon juice
  30ml/2 tbsp tomato purée (paste)
  salt and ground black pepper
  lemon slices and mint sprigs,
   to garnish

1 Rinse the vine leaves well under cold running water, then drain. Bring a pan of lightly salted water to the boil. Add the rice, lower the heat, cover and simmer for 10–12 minutes, or until almost cooked. Drain.

2 Heat 10ml/2 tsp of the olive oil in a non-stick frying pan, add the onion and cook until soft. Stir in the pine nuts and cook until lightly browned, then add the raisins, chopped mint, cinnamon, allspice and sumac, with salt and pepper to taste. Stir in the rice and mix well. Leave to cool.

COOK'S TIP
Vacuum-packed vine leaves are available from Cypriot and Middle Eastern food stores, as well as some delicatessens.

3 Line a pan with any damaged vine leaves. Trim the stalks from the remaining leaves and lay them flat. Place a little filling on each. Fold the sides over and roll up each leaf neatly. Place the dolmades side by side in the leaf-lined pan, so that they fit tightly.

4 Mix 300ml/½ pint/1¼ cups water with the lemon juice and tomato purée in a bowl. Whisk in the remaining olive oil. Pour the mixture over the dolmades and place a heatproof plate on top to keep them in place.

5 Cover the pan and simmer the dolmades for about 1 hour, or until all the liquid has evaporated and the leaves are tender. Transfer to a platter, garnish with lemon slices and mint sprigs and serve hot or cold.

VARIATION
Fresh vine leaves may be used but must be blanched in boiling water first to make them pliable.

Energy 52kcal/216kJ; Protein 1g; Carbohydrate 6.1g, of which sugars 2.4g; Fat 2.6g, of which saturates 0.2g, of which polyunsaturates 1.1g; Cholesterol 0mg; Calcium 12mg; Fibre 0.3g; Sodium 6mg.

TSATZIKI ★

YOU CAN SERVE THIS REDUCED-FAT VERSION OF THE CLASSIC GREEK DIP WITH STRIPS OF PITTA BREAD TOASTED ON THE BARBECUE, OR YOU COULD USE VEGETABLE STRIPS. THE TANGY CUCUMBER MAKES IT A LIGHT, REFRESHING SNACK FOR WARM SUMMER DAYS.

2 Trim the spring onions and garlic, then chop both very finely.

3 Beat the yogurt in a bowl until smooth, if necessary, then gently stir in the chopped cucumber, spring onions, garlic and mint until well combined.

4 Add salt and plenty of ground black pepper to taste, then transfer the mixture to a serving bowl. Chill in the refrigerator until ready to serve, then garnish with a small mint sprig. Serve the dip with slices of pitta bread that have been toasted on the barbecue.

SERVES FOUR

INGREDIENTS
    1 mini cucumber
    4 spring onions (scallions)
    1 garlic clove
    200ml/7fl oz/scant 1 cup low-fat
      Greek (US strained plain) yogurt
    45ml/3 tbsp chopped fresh mint
    salt and ground black pepper
    fresh mint sprig, to garnish (optional)
    toasted pitta bread, to serve

1 Trim the ends from the cucumber, then cut it into 5mm/¼in dice.

Energy 76kcal/316kJ; Protein 3.7g; Carbohydrate 3.7g, of which sugars 2.9g; Fat 5g, of which saturates 3.4g, of which polyunsaturates 0.2g; Cholesterol 8mg; Calcium 95mg; Fibre 0.3g; Sodium 36mg.

BYESAR ★

BYESAR IS SIMILAR TO HUMMUS IN CONSISTENCY, BUT USES BROAD BEANS INSTEAD OF CHICKPEAS. IT IS EATEN BY DIPPING A MEDITERRANEAN-TYPE BREAD INTO GROUND SPICES AND THEN SCOOPING UP THE PURÉE. THIS LOW-FAT VERSION IS HARD TO BEAT FOR A TASTY APPETIZER.

SERVES EIGHT

INGREDIENTS

115g/4oz dried broad (fava)
  beans, soaked
2 garlic cloves, peeled
5ml/1 tsp cumin seeds
45ml/3 tbsp olive oil
salt, to taste
mint sprigs, to garnish
extra cumin seeds, cayenne pepper
  and fresh bread, to serve

COOK'S TIP
To soak dried beans, rinse them in a sieve (strainer) under the cold tap, then place them in a large bowl. Cover with plenty of cold water and leave to soak.

1 Put the beans in a pan with the whole garlic cloves and cumin seeds and add enough water just to cover. Bring to the boil, then reduce the heat and simmer until the beans are tender. Drain, cool and then slip off and discard the outer skin of each bean.

2 Place the beans in a blender or food processor and process, adding the oil and sufficient water to give a smooth soft dip. Season to taste with salt. Garnish with mint sprigs; serve with extra cumin seeds, cayenne pepper and plenty of fresh bread.

Energy 63kcal/261kJ; Protein 2.5g; Carbohydrate 3.7g, of which sugars 0.4g; Fat 4.3g, of which saturates 0.6g, of which polyunsaturates 0.4g; Cholesterol 0mg; Calcium 19mg; Fibre 2g; Sodium 3mg.

CANNELLINI BEAN AND SUN-DRIED TOMATO BRUSCHETTA ★

THIS TRADITIONAL ITALIAN-STYLE DISH IS A SOPHISTICATED VERSION OF CANNED BEANS ON TOAST. THE BEANS ADD FLAVOUR WHILE MAKING THIS APPETIZER MORE SUBSTANTIAL AND FILLING, BUT THEY ARE STILL LOW IN FAT. EAT IT AT ANY TIME OF DAY.

SERVES SIX

INGREDIENTS
150g/5oz/¾ cup dried
  cannellini beans
5 tomatoes
10ml/2 tsp olive oil
2 sun-dried tomatoes in oil,
  drained and finely chopped
2 garlic cloves
30ml/2 tbsp chopped fresh
  rosemary
12 slices Italian-style bread,
  such as ciabatta
salt and ground black pepper
a handful of fresh basil leaves,
  to garnish

VARIATION
Make the tomato base as in steps 2 and 3 and mix with olives instead of the beans.

1 Soak the beans in water overnight. Drain and rinse, place in a pan and cover with water. Bring to the boil, boil rapidly for 10 minutes. Reduce the heat and simmer for 50–60 minutes. Drain.

2 Meanwhile, place the tomatoes in a bowl, cover with boiling water, leave for 30 seconds, then refresh in cold water. Skin, seed and chop the flesh.

3 Heat the oil in a pan and add the fresh and sun-dried tomatoes. Crush 1 garlic clove and add it to the pan with the rosemary. Cook for 2 minutes.

4 Add the tomato mixture to the cooked cannellini beans, season to taste with salt and ground black pepper, and mix well. Heat through gently.

5 Preheat the grill (broiler) to high. Cut the remaining garlic clove in half and rub the cut sides of the bread slices with it. Toast the bread lightly on both sides. Spoon the cannellini bean mixture on top of the toast. Sprinkle with basil leaves to garnish and serve immediately.

COOK'S TIP
Canned beans can be used instead of dried; use 275g/10oz/2 cups drained, canned beans and add to the tomato mixture in step 4. If the beans are in brine, rinse and drain well before use.

Energy 284kcal/1203kJ; Protein 12.7g; Carbohydrate 49.7g, of which sugars 5.3g; Fat 5g, of which saturates 0.7g, of which polyunsaturates 1.5g; Cholesterol 0mg; Calcium 127mg; Fibre 5.1g; Sodium 376mg.

SUN-DRIED TOMATO, BASIL AND OLIVE PIZZA BITES ★

THIS RECIPE USES SCONE PIZZA DOUGH WITH THE ADDITION OF CHOPPED FRESH BASIL TO CREATE THE BASIS FOR THESE TASTY LOW-FAT APPETIZERS.

MAKES TWENTY-FOUR

INGREDIENTS

For the scone dough
115g/4oz/1 cup self-raising
(self-rising) flour
115g/4oz/1 cup self-raising
(self-rising) wholemeal
(whole-wheat) flour
pinch of salt
9–10 fresh basil leaves
50g/2oz/¼ cup butter, diced
about 150ml/¼ pint/⅔ cup
semi-skimmed (low-fat) milk

For the tomato sauce
10ml/2 tsp olive oil
1 onion, finely chopped
1 garlic clove, crushed
400g/14oz can chopped tomatoes
15ml/1 tbsp tomato purée (paste)
15ml/1 tbsp chopped fresh mixed
herbs, such as parsley, thyme, basil
and oregano
pinch of granulated sugar
salt and ground black pepper

For the topping
15ml/1 tbsp tomato oil (from the jar
of sun-dried tomatoes)
115g/4oz (drained weight) sun-dried
tomatoes in oil, chopped
10 pitted black olives, chopped
9–10 fresh basil leaves, shredded
50g/2oz reduced-fat mozzarella
cheese, grated
30ml/2 tbsp freshly grated
Parmesan cheese
extra shredded fresh basil leaves,
to garnish

1 Preheat the oven to 220°C/425°F/ Gas 7. To make the dough, mix together the flours and salt in a bowl. Tear the basil leaves into small pieces and add to the flour mixture. Rub in the butter until the mixture resembles fine breadcrumbs. Stir in enough milk to form a soft dough.

2 Knead the dough gently on a lightly floured surface. Roll out and use to line a 30 x 18cm/12 x 7in Swiss roll tin (jelly roll pan). Push up the edges of the dough to make a thin rim. Set aside.

3 To make the tomato sauce, heat the oil in a non-stick pan, add the onion and garlic and cook gently for about 5 minutes, until softened. Add the tomatoes, tomato purée, chopped herbs, sugar and seasoning. Simmer uncovered, stirring occasionally, for 15–20 minutes, or until the tomatoes have reduced to a thick pulp. Leave to cool slightly.

4 For the topping, brush the scone base with 7.5ml/1½ tsp of the tomato oil, then spread over the tomato sauce. Scatter over the sun-dried tomatoes, olives and shredded basil leaves.

5 Mix together the mozzarella and Parmesan cheeses and sprinkle over the top. Drizzle over the remaining tomato oil. Bake for about 20 minutes.

6 Cut lengthways and across into 24 bitesize pieces. Garnish with the extra shredded basil leaves and serve immediately.

Energy 73kcal/307kJ; Protein 2.4g; Carbohydrate 8g, of which sugars 1.4g; Fat 3.7g, of which saturates 1.9g, of which polyunsaturates 0.3g; Cholesterol 7mg; Calcium 42mg; Fibre 0.9g; Sodium 69mg.

SALADS AND SIDE DISHES

*The Mediterranean climate is ideal for growing
many different vegetables, especially the salad
varieties. Because they receive plenty of sun, they
grow large and have an intense and delicious
flavour. Choose from the healthy selection of
dishes in this chapter for a tasty light lunch or a
mouthwatering accompaniment to a meal.*

SWEET AND SOUR ARTICHOKE SALAD ★

AGRODOLCE IS A SWEET-AND-SOUR SAUCE THAT WORKS PERFECTLY IN THIS TASTY SALAD.

SERVES FOUR

INGREDIENTS
6 small globe artichokes
juice of 1 lemon
10ml/2 tsp olive oil
2 onions, roughly chopped
175g/6oz/1 cup fresh or frozen broad
  (fava) beans (shelled weight)
175g/6oz/1½ cups fresh or frozen
  peas (shelled weight)
salt and ground black pepper
fresh mint leaves, to garnish
For the *salsa agrodolce*
120ml/4fl oz/½ cup white
  wine vinegar
15ml/1 tbsp caster (superfine) sugar
handful of fresh mint leaves,
  roughly torn

1 Peel and discard the outer leaves from the artichokes, then cut the artichokes into quarters. Place them in a bowl of cold water with the lemon juice. Set aside.

2 Heat the oil in a large, non-stick pan, add the onions and cook gently until the onions are golden. Add the broad beans and stir, then drain the artichokes and add to the pan. Pour in about 300ml/½ pint/1¼ cups of water and cook, covered, for 10–15 minutes.

3 Add the peas, season with salt and pepper and cook, stirring occasionally, for a further 5 minutes, or until the vegetables are tender. Strain the mixture through a sieve, then place all the vegetables in a bowl. Leave to cool, then cover and chill in the refrigerator. Discard the cooking juices.

4 To make the *salsa agrodolce*, mix all the ingredients in a small pan. Heat gently, stirring, for 2–3 minutes, or until the sugar has dissolved, then simmer gently for about 5 minutes, stirring occasionally. Remove the pan from the heat and leave to cool. To serve, drizzle the salsa over the vegetables and garnish with fresh mint leaves.

Energy 138kcal/577kJ; Protein 8.6g; Carbohydrate 20.4g, of which sugars 10.1g; Fat 3g, of which saturates 0.4g, of which polyunsaturates 0.8g; Cholesterol 0mg; Calcium 157mg; Fibre 7.8g; Sodium 128mg.

MOROCCAN COOKED SALAD ★

THIS SALAD IS OFTEN SERVED WITH A MAIN COURSE. KEEPING IT FOR A DAY IMPROVES THE FLAVOUR.

SERVES SIX

INGREDIENTS
 2 well-flavoured tomatoes, quartered
 2 onions, chopped
 ½ cucumber, halved lengthways,
  seeded and sliced
 1 green (bell) pepper, halved, seeded
  and chopped
 30ml/2 tbsp lemon juice
 30ml/2 tbsp olive oil
 2 garlic cloves, crushed
 30ml/2 tbsp chopped fresh coriander
  (cilantro)
salt and ground black pepper
sprigs of fresh coriander (cilantro),
  to garnish

1 Put the tomatoes, onions, cucumber and green pepper into a pan. Add 60ml/4 tbsp water and bring to the boil, then reduce the heat and simmer for 5 minutes. Remove the pan from the heat and leave to cool.

2 In a small bowl, whisk together the lemon juice, olive oil and garlic. Strain the vegetables, then transfer them to a bowl. Pour over the dressing, season with salt and pepper and stir in the chopped coriander. Serve at once, garnished with coriander sprigs.

Energy 67Kcal/279kJ; Protein 1.6g; Carbohydrate 6.5g, of which sugars 5.2g; Fat 4.1g, of which saturates 0.6g, of which polyunsaturates 0.5g; Cholesterol 0mg; Calcium 40mg; Fibre 2.1g; Sodium 10mg.

COUSCOUS SALAD ★

THIS IS A SPICY LOW-FAT VARIATION ON THE CLASSIC MIDDLE EASTERN DISH KNOWN AS TABBOULEH, WHICH IS TRADITIONALLY MADE WITH BULGUR WHEAT, NOT COUSCOUS. THE INCLUSION OF PARSLEY AND MINT IN THIS DISH GIVES IT A DELICIOUS AND REFRESHING FLAVOUR.

SERVES FOUR

INGREDIENTS

15ml/1 tbsp olive oil
5 spring onions (scallions), chopped
1 garlic clove, crushed
5ml/1 tsp ground cumin
350ml/12fl oz/1½ cups
  vegetable stock
175g/6oz/1 cup couscous
2 tomatoes, peeled and chopped
60ml/4 tbsp chopped fresh parsley
60ml/4 tbsp chopped fresh mint
1 fresh green chilli, seeded and
  finely chopped
30ml/2 tbsp lemon juice
salt and ground black pepper
toasted pine nuts and grated lemon
  rind, to garnish
crisp lettuce leaves, to serve

1 Heat the oil in a non-stick pan. Add the spring onions, garlic and cumin and cook, stirring, for 1 minute. Add the stock and bring to the boil.

2 Remove the pan from the heat, stir in the couscous, cover the pan and leave it to stand for 10 minutes, or until the couscous has swelled and all the liquid has been absorbed. If using instant couscous, follow the instructions on the packet.

3 Turn the couscous into a bowl. Stir in the tomatoes, chopped parsley and mint, chilli and lemon juice, with salt and pepper to taste. If possible, leave to stand in a cool place for up to 1 hour to allow the flavours to develop fully.

4 To serve, line a bowl with lettuce leaves and spoon the couscous salad into the centre. Sprinkle the toasted pine nuts and grated lemon rind over, to garnish.

COOK'S TIP
Wash your hands thoroughly after preparing fresh chillies (or wear disposable gloves), as chillies contain oils which will irritate the skin and eyes.

Energy 142Kcal/594kJ; Protein 3.7g; Carbohydrate 24.9g, of which sugars 2.4g; Fat 3.7g, of which saturates 0.5g, of which polyunsaturates 0.4g; Cholesterol 0mg; Calcium 57mg; Fibre 1.7g; Sodium 12mg.

CARROT AND CUMIN SALAD ★

IN THIS LOW-FAT SALAD THE CARROTS ARE COOKED BEFORE BEING TOSSED IN VINAIGRETTE.
CUMIN HAS A SPICY AROMA AND A PUNGENT FLAVOUR THAT GOES WELL WITH ROOT VEGETABLES.
SERVE CHILLED FOR A FLAVOURSOME AND COOLING TREAT.

SERVES SIX

INGREDIENTS

    4 carrots, thinly sliced
    1.5ml/¼ tsp ground cumin, or to taste
    60ml/4 tbsp low-fat or fat-free
      garlic-flavoured vinaigrette-style
      salad dressing
    30ml/2 tbsp chopped fresh coriander
      (cilantro) leaves, or a mixture of
      fresh coriander and fresh parsley
    salt and ground black pepper

COOK'S TIP

There is a good range of low-fat and fat-free salad dressings available – choose one to suit your taste.

1 Cook the carrots by either steaming or boiling them in a pan of lightly salted water, until they are just tender but not soft. Drain them, leave for a few minutes to dry and cool, then pour them into a mixing bowl.

2 Add the cumin, garlic salad dressing and chopped herbs. Season to taste and chill well before serving. Check the seasoning just before serving and add more ground cumin, salt or black pepper, if required.

Energy 19Kcal/81kJ; Protein 0.5g; Carbohydrate 3g, of which sugars 2.5g; Fat 0.7g, of which saturates 0.1g, of which polyunsaturates 0.1g; Cholesterol 0mg; Calcium 24mg; Fibre 0.8g; Sodium 10mg.

BEETROOT WITH FRESH MINT ★

THIS SIMPLE AND DECORATIVE BEETROOT SALAD CAN BE SERVED AS PART OF A SELECTION OF SALADS, AS AN APPETIZER, OR AS AN ACCOMPANIMENT TO THE MAIN COURSE.

SERVES SIX

INGREDIENTS
    6 cooked beetroot (beets), peeled
    30ml/2 tbsp balsamic vinegar
    30ml/2 tbsp olive oil
    1 bunch fresh mint, leaves stripped
      and thinly shredded
    salt, to taste

VARIATION
To make Tunisian beetroot, add a little harissa to taste and substitute chopped fresh coriander (cilantro) for the shredded mint.

1 Slice the beetroot or cut into even-size dice with a sharp knife. Put the beetroot in a bowl. Add the balsamic vinegar, olive oil and a pinch of salt and toss together to combine.

2 Add half the thinly shredded mint to the salad and toss lightly until thoroughly combined. Chill the salad in the refrigerator for about 1 hour. Serve garnished with the remaining shredded mint leaves.

Energy 58kcal/240kJ; Protein 1.4g; Carbohydrate 4.8g, of which sugars 4.1g; Fat 3.8g, of which saturates 0.5g, of which polyunsaturates 0.4g; Cholesterol 0mg; Calcium 29mg; Fibre 0.9g; Sodium 53mg.

BLACK AND ORANGE SALAD ★

THIS DRAMATIC SALAD IS TYPICALLY MOROCCAN — THE DARK BLACK OLIVES CONTRASTING IN TASTE AND COLOUR WITH THE SWEET ORANGES, A FAVOURITE MOROCCAN FRUIT.

SERVES FOUR

INGREDIENTS
3 oranges
60g/2oz pitted black olives
15ml/1 tbsp chopped fresh
  coriander (cilantro)
15ml/1 tbsp chopped fresh parsley
30ml/2 tbsp olive oil
15ml/1 tbsp lemon juice
2.5ml/½ tsp paprika
2.5ml/½ tsp ground cumin

COOK'S TIP
Use a sharp serrated knife to cut away the white pith from the orange flesh.

1 Cut away the peel and pith from the oranges and cut the flesh into wedges.

2 Place the oranges in a salad bowl and add the black olives, chopped coriander and parsley.

3 In a small bowl, whisk together the olive oil, lemon juice, paprika and cumin. Pour the dressing over the salad and toss gently to mix. Chill in the refrigerator for about 30 minutes before serving.

Energy 77Kcal/323kJ; Protein 1.5g; Carbohydrate 8g, of which sugars 7.9g; Fat 4.6g, of which saturates 0.7g, of which polyunsaturates 0.4g; Cholesterol 0mg; Calcium 74mg; Fibre 2.5g; Sodium 346mg.

PATATAS BRAVAS ★

THERE ARE SEVERAL VARIATIONS ON THIS CHILLI AND POTATO DISH, BUT THE MOST IMPORTANT THING IS THE SPICING, WHICH IS MADE HOTTER STILL BY ADDING VINEGAR. THE CLASSIC VERSION IS MADE WITH FRESH TOMATO SAUCE FLAVOURED WITH GARLIC AND CHILLI.

SERVES FOUR

INGREDIENTS
  675g/1½lb small new potatoes
  25ml/1½ tbsp olive oil
  2 garlic cloves, sliced
  3 dried chillies, seeded
    and chopped
  2.5ml/½ tsp ground cumin
  10ml/2 tsp paprika
  30ml/2 tbsp red or white
    wine vinegar
  1 green or red (bell) pepper,
    seeded and sliced
  coarse sea salt, for sprinkling
    (optional)

1 Scrub the potatoes and put them into a pan of salted water. Bring to the boil and cook for 10 minutes, or until almost tender. Drain and leave to cool slightly. Peel, if you like, then cut into chunks.

2 Heat the oil in a large non-stick frying or sauté pan and fry the potatoes, turning them frequently, until golden.

3 Meanwhile, crush together the garlic, chillies and cumin using a mortar and pestle. Mix the paste with the paprika and wine vinegar, then add to the potatoes with the sliced pepper and cook, stirring, for 2 minutes. Sprinkle with salt, if using, and serve hot as a tapas dish or cold as a side dish.

Energy 173kcal/728kJ; Protein 3.3g; Carbohydrate 30g, of which sugars 4.9g; Fat 5g, of which saturates 0.9g, of which polyunsaturates 0.6g; Cholesterol 0mg; Calcium 14mg; Fibre 2.4g; Sodium 20mg.

MOJETE ★

The Spanish love to scoop up cooked vegetables with bread, and the name of this dish, which is derived from the word meaning to dip, reflects that. Peppers, tomatoes and onions are baked together to make a colourful, low-fat soft vegetable dish.

SERVES EIGHT

INGREDIENTS

2 red (bell) peppers
2 yellow (bell) peppers
1 red onion, sliced
2 garlic cloves, halved
50g/2oz/⅓ cup black olives
6 large ripe tomatoes, quartered
5ml/1 tsp soft light brown sugar
45ml/3 tbsp amontillado sherry
3–4 fresh rosemary sprigs
25ml/1½ tbsp olive oil
salt and ground black pepper
fresh bread, to serve (optional)

1 Halve the peppers lengthways and remove and discard the stalks, cores and seeds. Cut each pepper lengthways into 12 even strips. Preheat the oven to 200°C/400°F/Gas 6.

2 Place the peppers, onion, garlic, olives and tomatoes in a large non-stick roasting pan. Sprinkle the vegetables with the sugar, then pour in the sherry. Season well with salt and pepper, cover with foil and bake in the oven for 45 minutes.

3 Remove the foil from the pan and stir the mixture well. Add the rosemary sprigs and drizzle with the olive oil. Return the pan to the oven and bake, uncovered, for a further 30 minutes, or until the vegetables are very tender. Serve hot or cold with plenty of chunks of fresh crusty bread, if you like.

COOK'S TIP
Spain is the world's chief olive producer, with half the crop being exported. Try to use good quality Spanish olives for this recipe. Choose unpitted ones as they have a better flavour.

Energy 76kcal/315kJ; Protein 1.4g; Carbohydrate 8.5g, of which sugars 8.1g; Fat 3.5g, of which saturates 0.6g, of which polyunsaturates 0.6g; Cholesterol 0mg; Calcium 18mg; Fibre 2.3g; Sodium 178mg.

SPICY ROASTED VEGETABLES ★

OVEN-ROASTING BRINGS OUT ALL THE FLAVOURS OF CHERRY TOMATOES, COURGETTES, ONION AND RED PEPPERS. SERVE THEM HOT FOR A DELICIOUS ACCOMPANIMENT TO THE MAIN MEAL.

SERVES FOUR

INGREDIENTS

2–3 courgettes (zucchini)
1 Spanish (Bermuda) onion
2 red (bell) peppers
16 cherry tomatoes
2 garlic cloves, chopped
pinch of cumin seeds
5ml/1 tsp chopped fresh thyme or
  4–5 torn fresh basil leaves
25ml/1½ tbsp olive oil
juice of ½ lemon
5–10ml/1–2 tsp harissa or
  Tabasco sauce
fresh thyme sprigs, to garnish

COOK'S TIP

Harissa is a chilli paste, popular in northern Africa. It can be bought in jars or cans and contains pounded chillies, garlic, coriander, olive oil and seasoning.

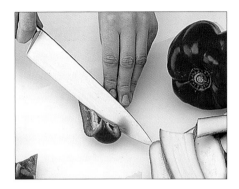

1 Preheat the oven to 220°C/425°F/ Gas 7. Trim the courgettes and cut into long strips. Cut the onion into thin wedges. Cut the peppers into chunks, discarding the stalks, cores and seeds.

2 Place these vegetables in a cast-iron dish or non-stick roasting pan; add the tomatoes, garlic, cumin seeds and chopped thyme or torn basil leaves.

3 Sprinkle with the olive oil and toss to coat. Roast the mixture in the oven for 25–30 minutes, or until the vegetables are very soft and have begun to char slightly.

4 In a cup, mix the lemon juice with the harissa or Tabasco sauce. Stir into the vegetables, garnish with the thyme sprigs and serve immediately.

Energy 117kcal/484kJ; Protein 4.1g; Carbohydrate 14g, of which sugars 11.3g; Fat 5g, of which saturates 0.8g, of which polyunsaturates 0.8g; Cholesterol 0mg; Calcium 77mg; Fibre 3.4g; Sodium 9mg.

TOMATOES WITH OKRA AND CORIANDER ★

OKRA IS FREQUENTLY COMBINED WITH TOMATOES AND MILD SPICES IN MEDITERRANEAN COUNTRIES.
LOOK FOR FRESH OKRA THAT IS SOFT AND VELVETY, NOT DRY AND SHRIVELLED.

SERVES FOUR

INGREDIENTS
  450g/1lb fresh tomatoes or
    400g/14oz can chopped tomatoes
  450g/1lb okra
  20ml/4 tsp olive oil
  2 onions, thinly sliced
  10ml/2 tsp coriander seeds, crushed
  3 garlic cloves, crushed
  2.5ml/½ tsp granulated sugar
  finely grated rind and juice of
    1 lemon
  salt and ground black pepper

COOK'S TIP
When okra pods are sliced, they ooze a sticky, somewhat mucilaginous liquid which, when cooked, acts as a thickener. It gives dishes a very distinctive texture, which not everyone appreciates. If the pods are left whole, however, as here, all you get is the delicious flavour.

1 If using fresh tomatoes, cut a cross in the base of each tomato, plunge them into a bowl of boiling water for 30 seconds, then refresh them in cold water. Peel off and discard the skins and roughly chop the tomato flesh. Set aside.

2 Trim off and discard any stalks from the okra and leave whole. Heat the oil in a non-stick frying pan and cook the onions and coriander seeds for 3–4 minutes, or until the onions are beginning to colour.

3 Add the okra and garlic to the pan and cook for 1 minute. Gently stir in the chopped fresh or canned tomatoes. Add the sugar, which will bring out the flavour of the tomatoes. Simmer gently for about 20 minutes, stirring once or twice, or until the okra is tender.

4 Stir in the lemon rind and juice, and add salt and pepper to taste, adding a little more sugar if necessary. Serve warm or cold.

Energy 88kcal/370kJ; Protein 4.1g; Carbohydrate 8.6g, of which sugars 7.7g; Fat 4.5g, of which saturates 0.9g, of which polyunsaturates 0.8g; Cholesterol 0mg; Calcium 192mg; Fibre 5.8g; Sodium 20mg.

OVEN-ROASTED RED ONIONS ★

THE WONDERFUL TASTE OF THESE APPETIZING SWEET RED ONIONS IS ENHANCED WITH THE POWERFUL COMBINATION OF FLAVOURS OF FRESH ROSEMARY, CRUSHED JUNIPER BERRIES, AND THE ADDED TANGY SWEETNESS FROM THE BALSAMIC VINEGAR.

SERVES FOUR

INGREDIENTS

4 large or 8 small red onions
25ml/1½ tbsp olive oil
6 juniper berries, crushed
8 small fresh rosemary sprigs
30ml/2 tbsp balsamic vinegar
salt and ground black pepper

VARIATION
Add a similar quantity of long, thin potato wedges to the onion. Use a larger dish so that the vegetables are still in one layer.

COOK'S TIP
If you don't have a clay onion baker, you can use any lidded ovenproof dish for this recipe.

1 Soak a clay onion baker in cold water for 15 minutes, then drain. If the base of the baker is glazed, only the lid will need to be soaked.

2 Trim and discard the roots from the onions and remove the skins, if you like. Cut the onions from the tip to the root, cutting the large onions into quarters and the small onions in half.

3 Lightly rub the onions with olive oil, salt and pepper and the juniper berries. Place the onions in the baker, inserting the rosemary in among the onions. Drizzle the remaining oil and vinegar over.

4 Cover and place in a cold oven. Set the oven to 200°C/400°F/Gas 6 and roast for 40 minutes. Remove the lid and roast for a further 10 minutes.

Energy 47kcal/194kJ; Protein 1.5g; Carbohydrate 9.9g, of which sugars 7.1g; Fat 0.3g, of which saturates 0g, of which polyunsaturates 0.1g; Cholesterol 0mg; Calcium 32mg; Fibre 1.8g; Sodium 4mg.

MARINATED MUSHROOMS ★

CHAMPIÑONES EN ESCABECHE *IS A GOOD WAY TO SERVE MUSHROOMS IN SUMMER, AND MAKES A REFRESHING LOW-FAT ALTERNATIVE TO THE EVER-POPULAR MUSHROOMS FRIED IN GARLIC. SERVE WITH PLENTY OF CRUSTY BREAD TO MOP UP THE DELICIOUS JUICES.*

SERVES FOUR

INGREDIENTS
    10ml/2 tsp olive oil
    1 small onion, very finely chopped
    1 garlic clove, finely chopped
    15ml/1 tbsp tomato purée (paste)
    50ml/2fl oz/¼ cup amontillado sherry
    50ml/2fl oz/¼ cup water
    2 cloves
    225g/8oz/3 cups button (white)
      mushrooms, trimmed
    salt and ground black pepper
    chopped fresh parsley, to garnish

VARIATION
In Spain, wild mushrooms, known as *setas*, are served in this way.

1 Heat the oil in a non-stick pan. Add the onion and garlic and cook until soft. Stir in the tomato purée, sherry, water and cloves and season with salt and black pepper. Bring to the boil, cover and simmer gently for 45 minutes, adding more water if it becomes too dry.

2 Add the mushrooms to the pan, then cover and simmer for about 5 minutes. Remove from the heat and allow to cool, still covered. Chill in the refrigerator overnight. Serve the mushrooms cold, sprinkled with the chopped parsley, to garnish.

Energy 44kcal/181kJ; Protein 1.4g; Carbohydrate 2.1g, of which sugars 1.7g; Fat 1.8g, of which saturates 0.3g, of which polyunsaturates 0.3g; Cholesterol 0mg; Calcium 9mg; Fibre 0.9g; Sodium 14mg.

BRAISED LETTUCE AND PEAS WITH MINT ★

BASED ON THE TRADITIONAL FRENCH WAY OF BRAISING PEAS WITH LETTUCE IN A LITTLE BUTTER, THIS LOW-FAT DISH IS DELICIOUS WITH AN OMELETTE OR PASTA-BASED MAIN COURSE.

SERVES SIX

INGREDIENTS
25g/1oz/2 tbsp butter
4 Little Gem (Bibb) lettuces,
  halved lengthways
2 bunches spring onions (scallions),
  cut into bitesize pieces
5ml/1 tsp granulated sugar
400g/14oz shelled peas (about
  1kg/2¼lb in pods)
4–5 fresh mint sprigs, plus extra
  to garnish
120ml/4fl oz/½ cup vegetable stock
salt and ground black pepper

2 Toss the vegetables in the butter, then sprinkle in the sugar, 2.5ml/½ tsp salt and plenty of black pepper. Cover, then cook very gently for 5 minutes, stirring once.

3 Add the peas and mint sprigs to the pan. Toss the peas in the juices, then pour in the stock.

4 Cover the pan and cook over a gentle heat for a further 5 minutes, or until the peas are almost tender, then remove the lid from the pan. Increase the heat to high and cook, stirring occasionally, until the cooking liquid has reduced to a few tablespoons.

5 Stir in the remaining butter and adjust the seasoning. Transfer to a warmed serving dish and garnish with the extra mint. Serve immediately.

VARIATIONS
• Braise about 250g/9oz baby carrots with the lettuce.
• Use 1 lettuce, shredding it coarsely, and omit the fresh mint. Towards the end of cooking, stir in about 150g/5oz rocket (arugula) – preferably the slightly stronger-flavoured, wild variety – and cook briefly until just wilted.

1 Melt half the butter in a wide, heavy non-stick pan over a low heat. Add the lettuces and spring onions.

Energy 110kcal/455kJ; Protein 6.2g; Carbohydrate 10.8g, of which sugars 4.3g; Fat 5g, of which saturates 2.5g, of which polyunsaturates 0.9g; Cholesterol 9mg; Calcium 64mg; Fibre 4.2g; Sodium 32mg.

BAKED VEGETABLE PANCAKE ★

CRUNCHY GOLDEN BATTER SURROUNDS THESE VEGETABLES, MAKING THEM DELICIOUS AND FILLING.
SERVE AS A SIDE DISH OR WITH SALAD AS A LIGHT LUNCH.

SERVES EIGHT

INGREDIENTS
  1 small aubergine (eggplant),
    trimmed, halved and thickly sliced
  1 egg
  115g/4oz/1 cup plain (all-purpose) flour
  300ml/½ pint/1¼ cups
    semi-skimmed (low-fat) milk
  30ml/2 tbsp fresh thyme,
    or 10ml/2 tsp dried
  1 red onion
  2 large courgettes (zucchini)
  1 red (bell) pepper
  1 yellow (bell) pepper
  30ml/2 tbsp sunflower oil
  30ml/2 tbsp freshly grated
    Parmesan cheese (optional)
  salt and ground black pepper
  fresh herbs, to garnish

1 Place the aubergine slices in a colander, sprinkle generously with salt and leave for 10 minutes. Drain, rinse well and pat dry on kitchen paper.

2 Meanwhile, beat the egg in a bowl, then gradually beat in the flour and a little milk to make a smooth, thick paste. Gradually blend in the rest of the milk, add the thyme and seasoning to taste and stir until smooth. Leave the batter in a cool place until required. Preheat the oven to 220°C/425°F/Gas 7.

COOK'S TIP
It is essential to get the fat in the dish really hot before adding the batter, which should sizzle slightly as it goes in. If the fat is not hot enough, the batter will not rise well.

3 Quarter the onion, trim and slice the courgettes, and seed and quarter the peppers. Put the oil in a non-stick roasting pan and heat in the oven until hot. Add the prepared vegetables, toss in the oil to coat thoroughly and return to the oven for 20 minutes.

4 Whisk the batter again, then pour over the vegetables. Return to the oven for 30 minutes. When puffed up and golden, reduce the heat to 190°C/375°F/Gas 5 for 10–15 minutes, or until crisp around the edges. Sprinkle with Parmesan, if using, garnish with herbs and serve.

Energy 124kcal/522kJ; Protein 5.1g; Carbohydrate 17.7g, of which sugars 6.3g; Fat 4.2g, of which saturates 0.7g, of which polyunsaturates 0.8g; Cholesterol 25mg; Calcium 90mg; Fibre 2.2g; Sodium 29mg.

COURGETTES IN TOMATO SAUCE ★

THIS RICHLY FLAVOURED MEDITERRANEAN DISH CAN BE SERVED HOT OR COLD AS AN ACCOMPANIMENT. CUT THE COURGETTES INTO FAIRLY THICK SLICES, SO THAT THEY STAY SLIGHTLY CRUNCHY.

SERVES FOUR

INGREDIENTS
    15ml/1 tbsp extra virgin olive oil
      or sunflower oil
    1 onion, chopped
    1 garlic clove, chopped
    4 courgettes (zucchini),
      thickly sliced
    400g/14oz can chopped tomatoes
    2 tomatoes, skinned, seeded
      and chopped
    5ml/1 tsp vegetable bouillon powder
    15ml/1 tbsp tomato purée (paste)
    salt and ground black pepper

1 Heat the oil in a heavy non-stick pan, add the onion and garlic and sauté, stirring occasionally, for 5 minutes, or until the onion is softened. Add the courgettes and cook, stirring occasionally, for a further 5 minutes.

2 Add the canned and fresh tomatoes, bouillon powder and tomato purée. Stir well, then simmer for 10–15 minutes, or until the sauce is thickened and the courgettes are just tender. Season to taste with salt and pepper and serve.

Energy 77kcal/320kJ; Protein 3.2g; Carbohydrate 8.2g, of which sugars 7.7g; Fat 3.7g, of which saturates 0.7g, of which polyunsaturates 0.8g; Cholesterol 0mg; Calcium 41mg; Fibre 2.7g; Sodium 24mg.

RATATOUILLE ★

A HIGHLY VERSATILE TOMATO AND MIXED VEGETABLE STEW FROM PROVENCE IN FRANCE, RATATOUILLE IS DELICIOUS SERVED WARM OR COLD. THIS LOW-FAT VERSION IS FULL OF FLAVOUR TOO!

SERVES SIX

INGREDIENTS
  900g/2lb ripe plum tomatoes
  30ml/2 tbsp olive oil
  2 onions, thinly sliced
  2 red and 1 yellow (bell) peppers,
    seeded and cut into chunks
  1 large aubergine (eggplant), cut
    into chunks
  2 courgettes (zucchini), sliced
  4 garlic cloves, crushed
  2 bay leaves
  15ml/1 tbsp chopped fresh thyme
  salt and ground black pepper

1 Plunge the tomatoes into boiling water for 30 seconds, then refresh in cold water. Peel away and discard the skins, then roughly chop the flesh.

2 Heat 10ml/2 tsp of the olive oil in a large, heavy non-stick pan and gently cook the onions for 5 minutes. Stir them constantly so that they do not brown, as this will adversely affect their flavour and make them bitter, but cook them until they are just transparent.

3 Add the peppers to the onions and cook for a further 2 minutes. Using a slotted spoon, transfer the onions and peppers to a plate and set them aside.

4 Add a further 10ml/2 tsp oil and the aubergine to the pan and cook gently for 5 minutes. Add the remaining oil and the courgettes, and cook for 3 minutes. Lift out the courgettes and aubergine and set them aside.

5 Add the garlic and tomatoes to the pan with the bay leaves and chopped thyme, and a little salt and pepper. Cook gently until the tomatoes have softened and are turning pulpy.

6 Return all the vegetables to the pan and cook gently, stirring frequently, for about 15 minutes, or until fairly pulpy but retaining a little texture. Adjust the seasoning to taste. Serve warm or cold.

Energy 120kcal/503kJ; Protein 4.1g; Carbohydrate 15.4g, of which sugars 14.4g; Fat 5g, of which saturates 0.9g, of which polyunsaturates 1.1g; Cholesterol 0mg; Calcium 48mg; Fibre 5.3g; Sodium 20mg.

ROASTED PLUM TOMATOES AND GARLIC ★

THESE ARE SO SIMPLE TO PREPARE YET TASTE ABSOLUTELY WONDERFUL. USE A LARGE, SHALLOW EARTHENWARE DISH THAT WILL ALLOW THE TOMATOES TO SEAR AND CHAR IN A HOT OVEN.

SERVES FOUR

INGREDIENTS
  8 plum tomatoes, halved
  12 garlic cloves
  20ml/4 tsp extra virgin olive oil
  3 bay leaves
  salt and ground black pepper
  45ml/3 tbsp fresh oregano leaves,
    to garnish

COOK'S TIP
Use ripe plum tomatoes for this recipe as they keep their shape and do not fall apart when roasted at such a high temperature. Leave the stalks on, if possible.

1 Preheat the oven to 230°C/450°F/Gas 8. Select an ovenproof dish that will hold all the tomatoes snugly in a single layer. Place the tomatoes in the dish and push the whole, unpeeled garlic cloves between them.

2 Lightly brush the tomatoes with the oil, add the bay leaves and sprinkle black pepper over the top. Bake in the oven for about 45 minutes, until the tomatoes have softened and are sizzling in the dish. They should be charred around the edges. Season with salt and a little more black pepper, if needed. Garnish with oregano leaves and serve at once.

Energy 70kcal/294kJ; Protein 1.8g; Carbohydrate 7.8g, of which sugars 7.8g; Fat 3.8g, of which saturates 0.7g, of which polyunsaturates 0.8g; Cholesterol 0mg; Calcium 18mg; Fibre 2.5g; Sodium 23mg.

GREEN BEANS WITH TOMATOES ★

THIS IS A REAL SUMMER FAVOURITE, USING THE BEST RIPE PLUM TOMATOES AND FRENCH BEANS. USE CRUSTY FRENCH BREAD TO MOP UP THE JUICES OF THIS FLAVOURFUL SALAD.

SERVES FOUR

INGREDIENTS
   5ml/1 tsp olive oil
   1 large onion, thinly sliced
   2 garlic cloves, finely chopped
   6 large ripe plum tomatoes, skinned,
      seeded and coarsely chopped
   150ml/¼ pint/⅔ cup dry white wine
   450g/1lb French (green) beans,
      sliced in half lengthways
   16 pitted black olives
   10ml/2 tsp lemon juice
   salt and ground black pepper

COOK'S TIPS
• French (green) beans need little
preparation and now that they are grown
without the string you simply trim them.
• When choosing, make sure that they
snap easily – this is a sign of freshness.

1 Heat the oil in a large, non-stick frying pan. Add the onion and garlic and cook for about 5 minutes, or until the onion is softened but not brown.

2 Add the chopped tomatoes, white wine, French beans, olives and lemon juice and cook over a gentle heat, stirring occasionally, for a further 20 minutes, or until the sauce is thickened and the beans are tender. Season to taste with salt and pepper and serve immediately.

Energy 122kcal/511kJ; Protein 4g; Carbohydrate 12.2g, of which sugars 10.4g; Fat 4.1g, of which saturates 0.7g, of which polyunsaturates 1.1g; Cholesterol 0mg; Calcium 78mg; Fibre 5.3g; Sodium 469mg.

MAIN COURSES

*This chapter provides a wide range of
nutritious, flavourful and satisfying dishes
that all the family will enjoy. Choose
from healthy hotpots, tempting pasta,
stuffed and roast vegetables, and lighter
versions of favourites such as Vegetable
Moussaka and Lasagne.*

ROASTED SQUASH ★★★

GEM SQUASH HAS A SWEET, SUBTLE FLAVOUR THAT CONTRASTS WELL WITH OLIVES AND SUN-DRIED TOMATOES IN THIS RECIPE. THE RICE ADDS SUBSTANCE WITHOUT CHANGING ANY OF THE FLAVOURS.

2 Mix together the rice, tomatoes, olives, goat's cheese, olive oil and chopped basil in a bowl.

3 Divide the rice mixture evenly between the squash and place them in a shallow non-stick baking tin (pan) or ovenproof dish, just large enough to hold the squash side by side.

SERVES TWO

INGREDIENTS
  4 whole gem squashes
  225g/8oz/2 cups cooked white
    long grain rice
  75g/3oz/1½ cups sun-dried
    tomatoes, chopped
  40g/1½ oz/⅓ cup pitted black
    olives, chopped
  50g/2oz/¼ cup soft goat's cheese
  10ml/2 tsp olive oil
  15ml/1 tbsp chopped fresh basil
    leaves, plus basil sprigs,
    to serve
  green salad, to serve (optional)

1 Preheat the oven to 180°C/350°F/ Gas 4. Trim away the base of each squash, slice off the top and scoop out and discard the seeds.

4 Cover with foil and bake in the oven for 45–50 minutes, or until the squash are tender when pierced with a skewer. Garnish with basil sprigs and serve with a green salad, if you like.

Energy 419kcal/1766kJ; Protein 15.7g; Carbohydrate 58.2g, of which sugars 18.4g; Fat 15g, of which saturates 6.6g, of which polyunsaturates 1.4g; Cholesterol 23mg; Calcium 359mg; Fibre 11.1g; Sodium 605mg.

PROVENÇAL STUFFED PEPPERS ★★★

THIS COLOURFUL MEDITERRANEAN DISH CREATES A TASTY LOW-FAT VEGETARIAN MEAL, IDEAL SERVED WITH A MIXED BABY LEAF SALAD AND CRUSTY BREAD.

SERVES FOUR

INGREDIENTS
  10ml/1 tsp olive oil
  1 red onion, sliced
  1 courgette (zucchini), diced
  115g/4oz mushrooms, sliced
  1 garlic clove, crushed
  400g/14oz can chopped tomatoes
  15ml/1 tbsp tomato purée (paste)
  40g/1½oz/scant ⅓ cup pine nuts
  30ml/2 tbsp chopped fresh basil
  4 large (bell) peppers
  50g/2oz/½ cup finely grated
    fresh Parmesan or half-fat Red
    Leicester cheese
  salt and ground black pepper
  fresh basil leaves, to garnish

1 Preheat the oven to 180°C/350°F/ Gas 4. Heat the oil in a non-stick pan, add the onion, courgette, mushrooms and garlic and cook gently, stirring occasionally, for 3 minutes.

2 Stir in the tomatoes and tomato purée, then bring to the boil and simmer uncovered, stirring occasionally, for 10–15 minutes, or until thickened slightly. Remove from the heat and stir in the pine nuts, chopped basil and seasoning.

COOK'S TIP
Leave the root end intact when slicing or dicing an onion. This will prevent the release of the strong juices and fumes that can cause eyes to water.

3 Cut the peppers in half lengthways and seed them. Blanch in a pan of boiling water for 3 minutes. Drain.

VARIATION
Use the vegetable sauce to stuff other vegetables, such as large courgettes or baby aubergines (eggplants), in place of the peppers.

4 Place the pepper halves, cut side up, in a shallow, ovenproof dish and fill with the vegetable mixture.

5 Cover the dish with foil and bake in the oven for 20 minutes. Remove the foil, sprinkle each pepper with a little grated cheese and bake, uncovered, for a further 5–10 minutes, or until the cheese is melted and bubbling. Garnish with basil leaves and serve at once.

Energy 223kcal/930kJ; Protein 10.4g; Carbohydrate 16.9g, of which sugars 15.9g; Fat 13.1g, of which saturates 3.5g, of which polyunsaturates 5g; Cholesterol 13mg; Calcium 190mg; Fibre 5g; Sodium 155mg.

BAKED CHEESE POLENTA WITH TOMATO SAUCE ★★★

POLENTA, OR CORNMEAL, IS A STAPLE FOOD IN ITALY THAT IS ALSO LOW IN FAT. IT IS COOKED LIKE A SORT OF PORRIDGE, AND EATEN SOFT, OR SET, CUT INTO SHAPES THEN BAKED OR GRILLED.

SERVES FOUR

INGREDIENTS

5ml/1 tsp salt
250g/9oz/2¼ cups quick-cook
  polenta
5ml/1 tsp paprika
2.5ml/½ tsp freshly grated nutmeg
10ml/2 tsp olive oil
1 large onion, finely chopped
2 garlic cloves, crushed
2 x 400g/14oz cans chopped
  tomatoes
15ml/1 tbsp tomato purée (paste)
5ml/1 tsp granulated sugar
salt and ground black pepper
75g/3oz/¾ cup Gruyère cheese,
  finely grated

1 Lightly grease an ovenproof dish and set aside. Line a 28 x 18cm/11 x 7in baking tin (pan) with clear film (plastic wrap). In a pan, bring 1 litre/1¾ pints/ 4 cups water to the boil with the salt.

2 Pour in the polenta in a steady stream and cook, stirring continuously, for 5 minutes. Beat in the paprika and nutmeg, then pour the mixture into the prepared tin and smooth the surface. Leave to cool.

3 Heat the oil in a non-stick pan and cook the onion and garlic until soft. Add the tomatoes, tomato purée and sugar. Season with salt and pepper. Bring to the boil, then reduce the heat and simmer for 20 minutes.

4 Meanwhile, preheat the oven to 200°C/400°F/Gas 6. Turn out the polenta on to a chopping board, and cut into 5cm/2in squares. Place half the squares in the prepared dish. Spoon over half the tomato sauce, and sprinkle with half the cheese. Repeat the layers. Bake in the oven for about 25 minutes, or until golden. Serve hot.

Energy 380kcal/1590kJ; Protein 15.2g; Carbohydrate 55.8g, of which sugars 9.5g; Fat 10.4g, of which saturates 4.3g, of which polyunsaturates 0.7g; Cholesterol 19mg; Calcium 250mg; Fibre 3.9g; Sodium 724mg.

RICH TOMATO AND MEDITERRANEAN VEGETABLE HOTPOT ★★

HERE'S A ONE-DISH MEDITERRANEAN MEAL THAT'S SUITABLE FOR FEEDING LARGE NUMBERS OF PEOPLE.
IT'S LOW IN FAT, LIGHTLY SPICED AND HAS PLENTY OF GARLIC — WHO COULD REFUSE?

SERVES FOUR

INGREDIENTS
- 30ml/2 tbsp extra virgin olive oil or sunflower oil
- 1 large onion, chopped
- 2 small–medium aubergines (eggplants), cut into small cubes
- 4 courgettes (zucchini), cut into small chunks
- 2 red, yellow or green (bell) peppers, seeded and chopped
- 115g/4oz/1 cup fresh or frozen peas
- 115g/4oz green beans
- 200g/7oz can flageolet or small cannellini beans, rinsed and drained
- 450g/1lb new or salad potatoes, peeled and cubed
- 2.5ml/½ tsp ground cinnamon
- 2.5ml/½ tsp ground cumin
- 5ml/1 tsp paprika
- 4–5 tomatoes, skinned
- 400g/14oz can chopped tomatoes
- 30ml/2 tbsp chopped fresh parsley
- 3–4 garlic cloves, crushed
- 350ml/12fl oz/1½ cups stock
- salt and ground black pepper
- black olives, to garnish
- fresh parsley, to garnish

1 Preheat the oven to 190°C/375°F/ Gas 5. Heat 15ml/1 tbsp of the oil in a heavy non-stick pan, and sauté the onion until golden. Add the aubergines, sauté for 3 minutes, then add the courgettes, peppers, peas, beans and potatoes, and stir in the spices and seasoning. Cook, stirring constantly, for 3 minutes.

2 Cut the fresh tomatoes in half and scoop out and discard the seeds. Chop the tomatoes finely and place them in a bowl. Stir in the canned tomatoes with the chopped parsley, garlic and the remaining olive oil. Spoon the aubergine mixture into a shallow ovenproof dish and level the surface.

3 Pour the stock over the aubergine mixture and then spoon the prepared tomato mixture over the top.

4 Cover the dish with foil and bake in the oven for 30–45 minutes, or until the vegetables are tender. Serve hot, garnished with black olives and parsley.

Energy 320kcal/1346kJ; Protein 13.4g; Carbohydrate 50.3g, of which sugars 22.8g; Fat 8.7g, of which saturates 1.6g, of which polyunsaturates 2.1g; Cholesterol 0mg; Calcium 105mg; Fibre 13.2g; Sodium 251mg.

Spinach with Beans, Raisins and Pine Nuts ★★★

This dish is traditionally made with chickpeas, but can also be made with haricot beans as here. Use either dried or canned beans.

SERVES FOUR

INGREDIENTS

115g/4oz/²⁄₃ cup haricot (navy) beans, soaked overnight, or 400g/14oz can, drained
30ml/2 tbsp olive oil
1 thick slice white bread
1 onion, chopped
3–4 tomatoes, skinned, seeded and chopped
2.5ml/½ tsp ground cumin
450g/1lb fresh spinach leaves
5ml/1 tsp paprika
1 garlic clove, halved
25g/1oz/3 tbsp raisins
15g/½oz pine nuts, toasted
salt and ground black pepper

1 Cook the dried beans in a pan of boiling water for about 1 hour, or until tender. Drain and set aside.

2 Heat 10ml/2 tsp of the oil in a frying pan and fry the bread until golden. Transfer to a plate and set aside.

3 Sauté the onion in a further 10ml/ 2 tsp of the oil over a gentle heat, until soft but not brown, then add the tomatoes and cumin and continue cooking over a gentle heat.

4 Wash the spinach thoroughly, removing any tough stalks. Heat the remaining oil in a large, non-stick pan, stir in the paprika and then add the spinach and 45ml/3 tbsp water. Cover and cook for a few minutes, or until the spinach has wilted.

5 Add the onion and tomato mixture to the spinach and stir in the haricot beans, then season with salt and pepper.

6 Place the garlic and fried bread in a blender or food processor and process until smooth. Stir the bread mixture into the spinach and bean mixture, together with the raisins. Add 175ml/6fl oz/ ¾ cup water and then cover and simmer very gently for 20–30 minutes, adding more water, if necessary.

7 Place the spinach mixture on a warmed serving plate and sprinkle with toasted pine nuts. Serve hot with Moroccan bread or other fresh bread.

Energy 251kcal/1051kJ; Protein 11.4g; Carbohydrate 28.2g, of which sugars 11g; Fat 11g, of which saturates 1.3g, of which polyunsaturates 3.6g; Cholesterol 0mg; Calcium 259mg; Fibre 7g; Sodium 217mg.

RED PEPPER RISOTTO ★

THIS DELICIOUS ITALIAN RISOTTO CREATES A FLAVOURFUL AND LOW-FAT SUPPER OR MAIN-COURSE DISH, IDEAL SERVED WITH A MIXED LEAF SALAD AND FRESH ITALIAN BREAD.

SERVES FOUR

INGREDIENTS
3 large red (bell) peppers
10ml/2 tsp olive oil
3 large garlic cloves, thinly sliced
400g/14oz can chopped tomatoes
225g/8oz can chopped tomatoes
2 bay leaves
about 1.2–1.5 litres/2–2½ pints/
  5–6¼ cups vegetable stock
450g/1lb/2¼ cups arborio rice or
  long grain brown rice
6 fresh basil leaves, shredded
salt and ground black pepper

1 Preheat the grill (broiler) to high. Put the peppers in a grill (broiling) pan and grill (broil) until the skins are blackened and blistered all over. Transfer the peppers to a bowl, cover with a clean, damp dish towel and leave for 10 minutes. Peel off and discard the skins, then slice the peppers, discarding the cores and seeds. Set aside.

2 Heat the oil in a wide, shallow, non-stick pan. Add the garlic and tomatoes and cook gently, stirring occasionally, for 5 minutes, then add the prepared pepper slices and the bay leaves. Stir well, then cook gently, stirring occasionally, for 15 minutes.

3 Pour the vegetable stock into a separate large, heavy pan and heat it to simmering point. Stir the rice into the vegetable mixture and cook for about 2 minutes, then add two or three ladlefuls of the hot stock. Cook, stirring occasionally, until all the stock has been absorbed into the rice.

4 Continue to add stock, making sure each addition has been absorbed before adding the next. When the rice is tender, season to taste.

5 Remove the pan from the heat, cover and leave to stand for 10 minutes. Remove and discard the bay leaves, then stir in the shredded basil. Serve.

Energy 490kcal/2052kJ; Protein 10.9g; Carbohydrate 103.8g, of which sugars 13.6g; Fat 3.1g, of which saturates 0.5g, of which polyunsaturates 0.7g; Cholesterol 0mg; Calcium 44mg; Fibre 3.9g; Sodium 20mg.

LENTIL FRITTATA ★★

THROUGHOUT THE MEDITERRANEAN A VARIETY OF THICK VEGETABLE OMELETTES ARE COOKED.
THIS TASTY SUPPER DISH COMBINES GREEN LENTILS, RED ONIONS, BROCCOLI AND CHERRY TOMATOES.

SERVES SIX

INGREDIENTS

  75g/3oz/scant ½ cup green lentils
  225g/8oz small broccoli florets
  2 red onions, halved and thickly sliced
  15ml/1 tbsp olive oil
  8 eggs
  45ml/3 tbsp water
  45ml/3 tbsp chopped fresh mixed
    herbs, such as oregano, parsley,
    tarragon and chives, plus extra
    sprigs to garnish
  175g/6oz cherry tomatoes, halved
  salt and ground black pepper

1 Place the lentils in a pan, cover with cold water and bring to the boil, then reduce the heat and simmer for 25 minutes until tender. Add the broccoli, return to the boil and cook for 1 minute.

VARIATIONS

Use green beans, halved, in place of broccoli florets. Use standard white onions in place of red onions.

2 Meanwhile place the onion slices and olive oil in a shallow earthenware dish or cazuela about 23–25cm/9–10in in diameter, and place in a cold (unheated) oven. Set the oven to 200°C/400°F Gas 6 and cook for 25 minutes.

3 In a bowl, whisk together the eggs, water, a pinch of salt and plenty of black pepper. Stir in the chopped herbs and set aside.

4 Drain the lentils and broccoli and stir into the onions. Add the cherry tomatoes and sir gently to combine.

5 Pour the egg mixture evenly over the vegetables. Reduce the oven temperature to 190°C/375°F/Gas 5. Return the dish to the oven and cook for 10 minutes, then push the mixture into the centre of the dish using a spatula, allowing the raw egg mixture in the centre to flow to the edges.

6 Return the dish to the oven and cook the frittata for a further 15 minutes, or until it is just set. Garnish with sprigs of fresh herbs and serve warm, cut into thick wedges.

Energy 182kcal/761kJ; Protein 14.2g; Carbohydrate 14.1g, of which sugars 5.7g; Fat 8.2g, of which saturates 2.2g, of which polyunsaturates 1.2g; Cholesterol 254mg; Calcium 99mg; Fibre 3.2g; Sodium 108mg.

VEGETABLE COUSCOUS ★★

A NORTH AFRICAN FAVOURITE THAT IS PERFECT FOR COOL SUMMER EVENINGS, THIS SPICY DISH MAKES AN EXCELLENT LOW-FAT AND NUTRITIOUS MEAL FOR THE FAMILY.

SERVES 4

INGREDIENTS

15ml/1 tbsp olive oil
1 onion, chopped
2 garlic cloves, crushed
5ml/1 tsp ground cumin
5ml/1 tsp paprika
400g/14oz can chopped tomatoes
300ml/½ pint/1¼ cups
  vegetable stock
1 cinnamon stick
generous pinch of saffron threads
4 baby aubergines (eggplants), quartered
8 baby courgettes (zucchini), trimmed
8 baby carrots
225g/8oz/1⅓ cups couscous
425g/15oz can chickpeas, rinsed
  and drained
175g/6oz/¾ cup pitted prunes
45ml/3 tbsp chopped fresh parsley
45ml/3 tbsp chopped fresh
  coriander (cilantro)
10–15ml/2–3 tsp harissa
salt, to taste

1 Heat the oil in a large non-stick pan. Add the onion and garlic and cook gently for 5 minutes, or until soft. Add the cumin and paprika and cook, stirring, for 1 minute.

2 Add the tomatoes, stock, cinnamon stick, saffron threads, aubergines, courgettes and carrots. Season with salt. Bring to the boil, then reduce the heat, cover and cook for 20 minutes until the vegetables are just tender.

3 Line a steamer, metal sieve (strainer) or colander with a double thickness of muslin (cheesecloth) and set aside. Soak the couscous according to the instructions on the packet. Add the chickpeas and prunes to the vegetables and cook for 5 minutes. Fork the couscous to break up any lumps and spread it in the prepared steamer. Place on top of the vegetables, cover, and cook for 5 minutes, or until hot.

4 Stir the chopped parsley and coriander into the vegetables. Heap the couscous on to a warmed serving plate. Using a slotted spoon, arrange the vegetables on top. Spoon over a little sauce and toss gently to combine. Stir the harissa into the remaining sauce and serve separately.

Energy 397kcal/1671kJ; Protein 14.8g; Carbohydrate 71.5g, of which sugars 26g; Fat 7.6g, of which saturates 1g, of which polyunsaturates 2.2g; Cholesterol 0mg; Calcium 137mg; Fibre 12g; Sodium 253mg.

BUTTER BEAN TAGINE ★★

SERVE THIS HEARTY AND HEALTHY MOROCCAN BUTTER BEAN DISH ON ITS OWN, OR WITH A LEAFY SALAD AND FRESH CRUSTY BREAD AS A MAIN MEAL.

SERVES FOUR

INGREDIENTS
  115g/4oz/⅔ cup butter (lima) beans,
    soaked overnight
  15ml/1 tbsp olive oil
  1 onion, chopped
  2–3 garlic cloves, crushed
  25g/1oz fresh root ginger, peeled
    and chopped
  pinch of saffron threads
  16 cherry tomatoes
  generous pinch of granulated sugar
  handful of fleshy black olives, pitted
  5ml/1 tsp ground cinnamon
  5ml/1 tsp paprika
  small bunch of chopped fresh
    flat leaf parsley
  salt and ground black pepper

1 Rinse the beans and place them in a large pan with plenty of fresh water. Bring to the boil and boil for about 10 minutes, then reduce the heat and simmer gently for 1–1½ hours, or until tender. Drain the beans and refresh under cold water.

2 Heat the olive oil in a heavy non-stick pan. Add the onion, garlic and ginger, and cook for about 10 minutes, or until softened but not browned. Stir in the saffron threads, followed by the cherry tomatoes and a sprinkling of sugar.

3 Continue to cook and as the tomatoes begin to soften, stir in the butter beans. When the tomatoes have heated through, stir in the olives, cinnamon and paprika. Season to taste with salt and pepper and sprinkle over the chopped parsley. Serve immediately.

COOK'S TIP
If you are in a hurry, you could use two 400g/14oz cans of butter (lima) beans for this tagine. Make sure you rinse the beans well and drain before adding them, as canned beans tend to be salty.

Energy 177kcal/742kJ; Protein 7.3g; Carbohydrate 18.8g, of which sugars 4.4g; Fat 8.7g, of which saturates 1.2g, of which polyunsaturates 1.6g; Cholesterol 0mg; Calcium 82mg; Fibre 5.2g; Sodium 861mg.

PARMIGIANA DI MELANZANE ★★

THIS SIMPLE DISH HAS ALL THE FLAVOURS OF TRADITIONAL ITALIAN INGREDIENTS. SERVE WITH A MIXED GREEN SALAD FOR A SUBSTANTIAL AND DELICIOUS, LOW-FAT SUPPER DISH.

SERVES EIGHT

INGREDIENTS
- 900g/2lb aubergines (eggplants), sliced lengthways
- 30ml/2 tbsp olive oil
- 600ml/1 pint/2½ cups garlic and herb passata (bottled strained tomatoes)
- 115g/4oz/1¼ cups freshly grated Parmesan cheese
- salt and ground black pepper

COOK'S TIP
Choose good-quality fresh Parmesan cheese (Parmigiano Reggiano is the best of Italy's Parmesan cheeses) for this recipe. Avoid the pre-grated long-life Parmesan cheeses, which are inferior in quality and flavour.

1 Preheat the grill (broiler) to high. Lightly brush the aubergine slices with the oil and season with salt and pepper to taste. Arrange the aubergine slices in a single layer on a grill (broiling) pan and grill (broil) for 4–5 minutes on each side, or until golden and tender. (You will have to do this in batches.)

VARIATION
For a delicious variation, layer a few artichoke hearts between the slices of aubergine.

2 Preheat the oven to 190°C/375°F/ Gas 5. Spoon a little passata into a large baking dish. Arrange a single layer of aubergine slices over the top and sprinkle with some grated Parmesan. Repeat the layers of passata, aubergine and Parmesan, until all the ingredients have been used up, finishing with a good sprinkling of Parmesan.

3 Bake in the oven for 20–25 minutes, or until golden and bubbling. Serve piping hot.

Energy 117kcal/490kJ; Protein 7.3g; Carbohydrate 4.7g, of which sugars 4.5g; Fat 7.9g, of which saturates 3.5g, of which polyunsaturates 0.6g; Cholesterol 14mg; Calcium 191mg; Fibre 2.7g; Sodium 332mg.

STUFFED TOMATOES <u>AND</u> PEPPERS ★★

COLOURFUL PEPPERS AND TOMATOES MAKE PERFECT CONTAINERS FOR VARIOUS VEGETABLE STUFFINGS. THIS LOW-FAT RICE AND HERB VERSION FROM GREECE USES TYPICALLY GREEK INGREDIENTS.

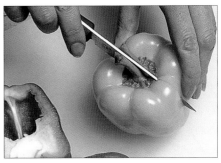

2 Halve the peppers lengthways, leaving the cores intact. Scoop out and discard the seeds. Brush the peppers with 10ml/2 tsp of the oil and bake in the oven on a baking sheet for 15 minutes. Place the peppers and tomatoes cut side up in a shallow ovenproof dish and season with salt and pepper. Set aside.

3 Heat the remaining oil in a non-stick frying pan and cook the onions for 5 minutes. Add the garlic and chopped almonds and cook for a further 1 minute.

4 Remove the pan from the heat and stir in the rice, chopped tomatoes, chopped mint and parsley, and sultanas. Season well with salt and pepper, then spoon the mixture into the tomatoes and peppers.

SERVES FOUR

INGREDIENTS
  2 large ripe tomatoes
  1 green (bell) pepper
  1 yellow or orange (bell) pepper
  20ml/4 tsp olive oil
  2 onions, chopped
  2 garlic cloves, crushed
  25g/1oz/¼ cup blanched
    almonds, chopped
  75g/3oz/scant ½ cup long grain rice,
    boiled and drained
  15g/½ oz chopped fresh mint
  15g/½ oz chopped fresh parsley
  25g/1oz sultanas (golden raisins)
  15g/½ oz ground almonds
  salt and ground black pepper
  chopped fresh mixed herbs, to garnish

1 Preheat the oven to 190°C/375°F/ Gas 5. Cut the tomatoes in half and scoop out the pulp and seeds using a teaspoon. Leave the tomatoes to drain on kitchen paper with cut sides down. Roughly chop the tomato pulp and seeds. Set aside.

5 Pour 150ml/¼ pint/⅔ cup boiling water around the tomatoes and peppers and bake, uncovered, in the oven for 20 minutes. Sprinkle with the ground almonds. Return to the oven and bake for a further 20 minutes, or until turning golden. Serve garnished with chopped mixed herbs.

Energy 234kcal/981kJ; Protein 5.7g; Carbohydrate 32.5g, of which sugars 14.5g; Fat 9.9g, of which saturates 1.2g, of which polyunsaturates 1.9g; Cholesterol 0mg; Calcium 71mg; Fibre 3.6g; Sodium 14mg.

MIXED MUSHROOM RISOTTO ★★

A CLASSIC RISOTTO OF MIXED MUSHROOMS, HERBS AND FRESH PARMESAN CHEESE, THIS IS BEST SIMPLY SERVED WITH A MIXED LEAF SALAD TOSSED IN A LIGHT FAT-FREE DRESSING.

SERVES FOUR

INGREDIENTS

15ml/1 tbsp olive oil
4 shallots, finely chopped
2 garlic cloves, crushed
10g/¼ oz dried porcini mushrooms,
 soaked in 150ml/¼ pint/⅔ cup hot
 water for 20 minutes
450g/1lb mixed mushrooms, such
 as closed cup, chestnut and field
 (portabello) mushrooms, sliced
250g/9oz/1¼ cups long grain rice
900ml/1½ pints/3¾ cups well-
 flavoured vegetable stock
30–45ml/2–3 tbsp chopped fresh
 flat leaf parsley
50g/2oz/⅔ cup freshly grated
 Parmesan cheese
salt and ground black pepper

1 Heat the oil in a large pan, then add the shallots and garlic and cook gently for 5 minutes, stirring continuously.

2 Drain the porcini, reserving their liquid, and chop roughly. Add all the mushrooms to the pan with the porcini soaking liquid, the rice and 300ml/ ½ pint/1¼ cups of the stock.

3 Bring to the boil, then reduce the heat and simmer uncovered, stirring frequently, until all the liquid has been absorbed. Add a ladleful of hot stock and stir until it has been absorbed.

4 Continue cooking and adding the hot stock, a ladleful at a time, stirring frequently, until the rice is cooked and creamy but *al dente*. This should take about 35 minutes and it may not be necessary to add all the stock.

5 Season to taste with salt and pepper, then stir in the chopped parsley and grated Parmesan and serve at once. Alternatively, sprinkle the Parmesan over the risotto just before serving.

Energy 328kcal/1386kJ; Protein 11.7g; Carbohydrate 52.8g, of which sugars 2.1g; Fat 9.3g, of which saturates 3.5g, of which polyunsaturates 1.3g; Cholesterol 13mg; Calcium 189mg; Fibre 3.2g; Sodium 148mg.

VEGETABLE MOUSSAKA ★★★

THIS IS A REALLY FLAVOURSOME, LOW-FAT VEGETARIAN ALTERNATIVE TO CLASSIC MEAT MOUSSAKA.
SERVE IT WITH WARM BREAD AND A GLASS OR TWO OF RUSTIC RED WINE.

SERVES SIX

INGREDIENTS
  450g/1lb aubergines
    (eggplants), sliced
  115g/4oz/½ cup dried whole
    green lentils
  600ml/1 pint/2½ cups
    vegetable stock
  1 bay leaf
  225g/8oz fresh tomatoes
  25ml/1½ tbsp olive oil
  1 onion, sliced
  1 garlic clove, crushed
  225g/8oz/3 cups mushrooms, sliced
  400g/14oz can chickpeas, rinsed
    and drained
  400g/14oz can chopped tomatoes
  30ml/2 tbsp tomato purée (paste)
  10ml/2 tsp dried basil
  300ml/½ pint/1¼ cups low-fat
    natural (plain) yogurt
  3 eggs
  50g/2oz/½ cup half-fat mature
    (sharp) Cheddar cheese, grated
  salt and ground black pepper
  fresh flat leaf parsley sprigs,
    to garnish

1 Sprinkle the aubergine slices with salt and place in a colander. Cover and leave over a sink for 30 minutes to allow any bitter juices to be extracted.

VARIATIONS
• Use brown cap (cremini), closed cup or button (white) mushrooms, or a mixture, for this recipe.
• Use canned borlotti, flageolet or cannellini beans in place of chickpeas.

2 Meanwhile, place the lentils, stock and bay leaf in a pan. Cover, bring to the boil and simmer for about 20 minutes, or until the lentils are just tender. Drain well and keep warm.

3 If you like, skin the fresh tomatoes, then roughly chop them.

4 Heat 10ml/2 tsp of the oil in a large, non-stick pan, add the onion and garlic, and cook, stirring, for 5 minutes. Stir in the lentils, mushrooms, chickpeas, fresh and canned tomatoes, tomato purée, basil and 45ml/3 tbsp water. Bring to the boil, cover and simmer gently for 10 minutes.

5 Preheat the oven to 180°C/350°F/ Gas 4. Rinse the aubergine slices, drain and pat dry. Heat the remaining oil in a non-stick frying pan and fry the slices in batches for 3–4 minutes, turning once.

6 Season the lentil mixture. Layer the aubergines and lentils in an ovenproof dish, starting with aubergines and finishing with the lentil mixture.

7 Beat together the yogurt, eggs and salt and pepper, and pour the mixture into the dish. Sprinkle with cheese and bake in the oven for 45 minutes. Serve, garnished with parsley sprigs.

Energy 285kcal/1202kJ; Protein 20.2g; Carbohydrate 29.6g, of which sugars 9.8g; Fat 10.5g, of which saturates 2.7g, of which polyunsaturates 2.2g; Cholesterol 99mg; Calcium 240mg; Fibre 7.5g; Sodium 306mg.

SPEEDY LASAGNE WITH MIXED MUSHROOMS AND PARMESAN ★★

THIS SIMPLE-TO-ASSEMBLE LOW-FAT VEGETARIAN VERSION OF LASAGNE REQUIRES NEITHER BAKING NOR THE LENGTHY PREPARATION OF VARIOUS SAUCES AND FILLINGS, BUT IS NO LESS DELICIOUS.

2 Heat the olive oil in a large, heavy non-stick frying pan and sauté the soaked mushrooms over a high heat for 5 minutes, or until the edges are slightly crisp. Reduce the heat, add the garlic and fresh mushrooms, and sauté for 5 minutes, stirring occasionally.

3 Add the wine and cook for 5–7 minutes, or until reduced. Stir in the tomatoes, sugar and seasoning and cook over a medium heat for about 5 minutes, or until thickened.

SERVES FOUR

INGREDIENTS
40g/1½oz/¾ cup dried porcini
  mushrooms
20ml/4 tsp olive oil
1 large garlic clove, chopped
375g/13oz mixed mushrooms,
  including brown cap (cremini),
  field (portabello), shiitake and
  wild varieties, roughly sliced
175ml/6fl oz/¾ cup dry white wine
90ml/6 tbsp canned chopped tomatoes
2.5ml/½ tsp granulated sugar
8 fresh lasagne sheets
40g/1½oz/½ cup freshly grated
  Parmesan cheese
salt and ground black pepper
fresh basil leaves, to garnish

1 Place the porcini mushrooms in a bowl and cover with boiling water. Leave to soak for 15 minutes, then drain and rinse. Set aside.

4 Meanwhile, cook the lasagne according to the instructions on the packet, until it is *al dente*. Drain lightly – the pasta should still be moist.

5 To serve, spoon a little of the mushroom sauce on to each of four warm serving plates. Place a sheet of lasagne on top and spoon a quarter of the remaining mushroom sauce over each serving. Sprinkle with some Parmesan and top with another pasta sheet. Sprinkle with black pepper and more Parmesan and garnish with basil leaves. Serve immediately.

Energy 117kcal/487kJ; Protein 5.8g; Carbohydrate 1.3g, of which sugars 1.2g; Fat 6.8g, of which saturates 2.6g, of which polyunsaturates 0.7g; Cholesterol 10mg; Calcium 131mg; Fibre 1.3g; Sodium 118mg.

FUSILLI WITH TOMATO AND BALSAMIC VINEGAR SAUCE ★★

THIS IS A MODERN ITALIAN-STYLE RECIPE. THE INTENSE, SWEET-SOUR FLAVOUR OF BALSAMIC VINEGAR GIVES A PLEASANT KICK TO A SAUCE MADE WITH CANNED TOMATOES.

SERVES SIX

INGREDIENTS
2 x 400g/14oz cans chopped Italian
    plum tomatoes
2 sun-dried tomatoes in oil, drained
    and thinly sliced
2 garlic cloves, crushed
30ml/2 tbsp olive oil
5ml/1 tsp granulated sugar
350g/12oz/3 cups fresh or
    dried fusilli
45ml/3 tbsp balsamic vinegar
salt and ground black pepper
rocket (arugula) salad and
    coarsely shaved Pecorino cheese,
    to serve (optional)

COOK'S TIP
Remember, the cooking time for fresh
and dried pasta is different – a shorter
cooking time for fresh pasta – so follow
the packet instructions carefully.

1 Put the canned and sun-dried tomatoes in a medium pan with the garlic, olive oil and sugar. Add salt and pepper to taste. Bring to the boil, stirring, then reduce the heat and simmer for about 30 minutes, or until reduced.

2 Meanwhile, cook the pasta in a pan of salted boiling water, according to the instructions on the packet.

3 Add the balsamic vinegar to the tomato sauce and stir to mix evenly. Cook for 1–2 minutes, then remove from the heat and adjust the seasoning to taste.

4 Drain the pasta and turn it into a warmed serving bowl. Pour the sauce over the pasta and toss well. Serve immediately, with a rocket salad and a little shaved Pecorino, if you like.

Energy 255kcal/1082kJ; Protein 7.9g; Carbohydrate 47.4g, of which sugars 6.1g; Fat 5.1g, of which saturates 0.8g, of which polyunsaturates 1g; Cholesterol 0mg; Calcium 24mg; Fibre 3g; Sodium 14mg.

CONCHIGLIE WITH ROASTED VEGETABLES ★★

NOTHING COULD BE SIMPLER — OR MORE DELICIOUS — THAN TOSSING FRESHLY COOKED PASTA WITH ROASTED VEGETABLES. THE FLAVOUR IS SUPERB AND THIS DISH IS LOW IN FAT TOO!

SERVES SIX

INGREDIENTS

1 red (bell) pepper, seeded and cut into 1cm/½in squares
1 yellow or orange (bell) pepper, seeded and cut into 1cm/½in squares
1 small aubergine (eggplant), roughly diced
2 courgettes (zucchini), roughly diced
30ml/2 tbsp extra virgin olive oil
15ml/1 tbsp chopped fresh flat leaf parsley
5ml/1 tsp dried oregano or marjoram
250g/9oz baby Italian plum tomatoes, hulled and halved lengthways
2 garlic cloves, roughly chopped
350–400g/12–14oz/3–3½ cups dried conchiglie
salt and ground black pepper
4–6 fresh marjoram or oregano flowers, to garnish

1 Preheat the oven to 190°C/375°F/ Gas 5. Rinse the prepared peppers, aubergine and courgettes in a colander under cold running water, drain well, then put the vegetables in a large, non-stick roasting pan.

2 Drizzle the olive oil over the vegetables and sprinkle with the chopped fresh and dried herbs. Add salt and pepper to taste and toss to mix well. Roast in the oven for about 30 minutes, stirring two or three times.

3 Stir the halved tomatoes and chopped garlic into the vegetable mixture, then roast for a further 20 minutes, stirring once or twice. Meanwhile, cook the pasta according to the instructions on the packet.

4 Drain the pasta and tip it into a warmed serving bowl. Add the roasted vegetables and any cooking juices and toss well. Serve the hot pasta and vegetables in warmed bowls, sprinkling each portion with a few herb flowers, to garnish.

Energy 281kcal/1188kJ; Protein 9.8g; Carbohydrate 50.8g, of which sugars 9.1g; Fat 5.7g, of which saturates 0.9g, of which polyunsaturates 1.2g; Cholesterol 0mg; Calcium 63mg; Fibre 5.1g; Sodium 13mg.

SPAGHETTI <u>WITH</u> FRESH TOMATO SAUCE ★★

THE HEAT FROM THE PASTA RELEASES THE DELICIOUS FLAVOURS OF THIS SAUCE. USE TRULY RIPE PLUM TOMATOES, AS THE AROMATIC QUALITY OF GOOD TOMATOES IMPROVES THE FLAVOUR OF THIS SAUCE.

SERVES FOUR

INGREDIENTS
  675g/1½lb ripe Italian
    plum tomatoes or sweet
    cherry tomatoes
  20ml/4 tsp extra virgin olive oil
    or sunflower oil
  1 onion, finely chopped
  350g/12oz fresh or dried spaghetti
  a small handful fresh basil leaves
  salt and ground black pepper
  coarsely shaved Parmesan cheese,
    to serve (optional)

COOK'S TIPS
• The Italian plum tomatoes called San Marzano are the best variety to use. When fully ripe, they have thin skins that peel off easily.
• In Italy, cooks often make this sauce in bulk in the summer months and freeze it for later use. Let it cool, then freeze in usable quantities in rigid containers. Thaw before reheating.

1 With a sharp knife, cut a cross in the base end of each tomato. Plunge the tomatoes, a few at a time, into a bowl of boiling water. Leave for 30 seconds or so, then lift them out with a slotted spoon and drop them into a bowl of cold water. Drain well. The skin will have begun to peel back from the crosses. Remove it entirely.

2 Place the tomatoes on a chopping board and cut into quarters, then eighths, and chop as finely as possible.

3 Heat the oil in a large non-stick pan, add the onion and cook over a low heat, stirring frequently, for about 5 minutes, or until softened and lightly coloured.

4 Add the tomatoes, season with salt and pepper to taste, bring to a simmer, then reduce the heat to low and cover the pan with a lid. Cook, stirring occasionally, for 30–40 minutes, or until the mixture is thick.

5 Meanwhile, cook the pasta in a separate pan, according to the instructions on the packet. Shred the basil leaves finely, or tear them into small pieces.

6 Remove the sauce from the heat, stir in the shredded basil and adjust the seasoning to taste. Drain the pasta, then tip the spaghetti into a warmed bowl, pour the sauce over and toss to mix well. Serve immediately, sprinkled with shaved fresh Parmesan, if you like.

Energy 360kcal/1531kJ; Protein 11.9g; Carbohydrate 71.3g, of which sugars 9g; Fat 5.1g, of which saturates 0.8g, of which polyunsaturates 1.3g; Cholesterol 0mg; Calcium 38mg; Fibre 4.4g; Sodium 18mg.

TAGLIATELLE ^{WITH} BROCCOLI ^{AND} SPINACH ★★

THIS IS AN EXCELLENT VEGETARIAN SUPPER DISH. IT IS NUTRITIOUS AND FILLING, AND NEEDS NO ACCOMPANIMENT. IF YOU LIKE, YOU CAN USE TAGLIATELLE FLECKED WITH HERBS.

SERVES FOUR

INGREDIENTS
    2 heads broccoli
    450g/1lb fresh spinach,
      stalks removed
    freshly grated nutmeg, to taste
    450g/1lb fresh or dried
      egg tagliatelle
    30ml/2 tbsp extra virgin olive oil
    juice of ½ lemon, or to taste
    salt and ground black pepper
    freshly grated Parmesan cheese,
      to serve (optional)

2 Add salt to the water in the steamer and top it up with boiling water, then add the pasta and cook according to the instructions on the packet. Meanwhile, chop the broccoli and spinach in the colander.

3 Drain the pasta. Heat the oil in the pasta pan, add the pasta and chopped vegetables and toss over a medium heat until evenly mixed. Sprinkle in the lemon juice and plenty of black pepper, then taste and add more lemon juice, salt and nutmeg, if you like. Serve immediately, sprinkled with black pepper and freshly grated Parmesan, if you like.

1 Put the broccoli in the basket of a steamer, cover and steam over a pan of boiling water for 10 minutes. Add the spinach to the broccoli, cover and steam for a further 4–5 minutes, or until both are tender. Towards the end of the cooking time, sprinkle the vegetables with freshly grated nutmeg and salt and pepper to taste. Transfer the vegetables to a colander and set aside.

VARIATIONS
• If you like, add a sprinkling of crushed dried chillies to the dish with the black pepper in step 3.
• To add both texture and protein, garnish the finished dish with one or two handfuls of toasted pine nuts. They are often served with broccoli and spinach in Italy. (Remember though, the addition of pine nuts will increase the fat content of the dish.)

Energy 520kcal/2199kJ; Protein 24.4g; Carbohydrate 88.3g, of which sugars 8g; Fat 10g, of which saturates 1.5g, of which polyunsaturates 2.8g; Cholesterol 0mg; Calcium 318mg; Fibre 10.2g; Sodium 175mg.

RIGATONI WITH TOMATOES AND MUSHROOMS ★★

THIS IS A GOOD SAUCE TO MAKE FROM STORE-CUPBOARD INGREDIENTS BECAUSE IT DOESN'T RELY ON ANYTHING FRESH, APART FROM THE SHALLOTS AND HERBS.

SERVES FOUR

INGREDIENTS

2 x 15g/½ oz packets dried
  wild mushrooms
175ml/6fl oz/¾ cup warm water
10ml/2 tsp olive oil
2 shallots, finely chopped
2 garlic cloves, crushed
a few sprigs fresh marjoram,
  chopped, plus extra to garnish
1 handful fresh flat leaf
  parsley, chopped
15g/½oz/1 tbsp cold butter
400g/14oz can chopped tomatoes
400g/14oz/3½ cups dried rigatoni
25g/1oz/⅓ cup freshly grated
  Parmesan cheese
salt and ground black pepper

1 Put the dried mushrooms in a bowl, pour the warm water over to cover and soak for 15–20 minutes. Turn into a fine sieve (strainer) set over a bowl and squeeze the mushrooms with your fingers to release as much liquid as possible. Reserve the mushrooms and the strained liquid.

2 Heat the oil in a non-stick frying pan and cook the shallots, garlic and chopped herbs over a low heat, stirring frequently, for about 5 minutes. Add the butter and soaked mushrooms, and stir until the butter has melted. Season well with salt and pepper.

3 Stir in the tomatoes and the reserved liquid from the soaked mushrooms. Bring to the boil, then reduce the heat, cover and simmer, stirring occasionally, for about 20 minutes. Meanwhile, cook the pasta according to the instructions on the packet.

4 Taste the sauce and adjust the seasoning. Drain the pasta, reserving some of the cooking water, and tip the pasta into a warmed large bowl. Add the sauce and the grated Parmesan and toss to mix. Add a little cooking water if you prefer a runnier sauce. Serve immediately, garnished with marjoram sprigs. Serve with more Parmesan cheese, which can be handed around separately, if you like.

VARIATION
If you have a bottle of wine open, red or white, add a splash when you add the canned tomatoes.

Energy 438kcal/1857kJ; Protein 15.8g; Carbohydrate 78.8g, of which sugars 7.6g; Fat 8.9g, of which saturates 3.8g, of which polyunsaturates 1.3g; Cholesterol 14mg; Calcium 137mg; Fibre 4.7g; Sodium 108mg.

DESSERTS
AND BREADS

In many Mediterranean countries, dessert often
comprises a simple serving of fresh fruit, but for
special occasions or a sweet treat, a number of low-
fat desserts can be enjoyed. Choose from frozen
delights such as Iced Clementines, or a rich, warm
Zabaglione. Finally, no meal is complete without
bread: try a traditional Focaccia or Panini all'Olio.

FRESH FIGS <u>WITH</u> HONEY <u>AND</u> WINE ★

ANY VARIETY OF FRESH FIGS CAN BE USED IN THIS TEMPTING LOW-FAT RECIPE, THEIR RIPENESS DETERMINING THE COOKING TIME.

SERVES SIX

INGREDIENTS
   450ml/¾ pint/scant 2 cups dry
    white wine
   75g/3oz/⅓ cup clear honey
   50g/2oz/¼ cup caster
    (superfine) sugar
   1 small orange
   8 whole cloves
   450g/1lb fresh figs
   1 cinnamon stick
   fresh mint sprigs or bay leaves,
    to decorate
   low-fat Greek (US strained plain)
    yogurt, to serve

VARIATION
Use fresh apricots or halved and stoned
(pitted) fresh peaches or nectarines in
place of figs.

1 Put the wine, honey and sugar in a heavy pan and heat gently, stirring constantly, until the sugar dissolves.

2 Stud the orange with the cloves and add to the syrup with the figs and cinnamon stick. Cover and simmer very gently for 5–10 minutes, or until the figs are softened. Transfer to a serving dish and leave to cool.

3 Decorate the figs with mint sprigs or bay leaves, then serve with low-fat Greek yogurt, if you like.

COOK'S TIP
Choose fresh figs that are plump and firm for this recipe, and use them quickly as they don't store well.

Energy 194kcal/822kJ; Protein 1.4g; Carbohydrate 36.4g, of which sugars 36.4g; Fat 0.5g, of which saturates 0g, of which polyunsaturates 0g; Cholesterol 0mg; Calcium 95mg; Fibre 2.5g; Sodium 26mg.

MOROCCAN DRIED FRUIT SALAD ★

THIS IS A WONDERFUL COMBINATION OF FRESH AND DRIED FRUIT AND MAKES AN EXCELLENT LIGHT DESSERT THROUGHOUT THE YEAR. USE FROZEN RASPBERRIES OR BLACKBERRIES IN WINTER.

SERVES FOUR

INGREDIENTS

115g/4oz/½ cup dried apricots
115g/4oz/½ cup dried peaches
1 fresh pear
1 fresh apple
1 fresh orange
115g/4oz/⅔ cup mixed raspberries
  and blackberries
1 cinnamon stick
50g/2oz/¼ cup caster
  (superfine) sugar
15ml/1 tbsp clear honey
30ml/2 tbsp lemon juice

1 Soak the apricots and peaches in a bowl of water for 1–2 hours or until plump, then drain and halve or quarter them. Set aside.

2 Peel and core the pear and apple and cut the flesh into cubes. Peel the orange with a sharp knife, removing all the white pith, and cut the flesh into wedges. Place all the fruit in a large pan with the raspberries and blackberries.

3 Add 600ml/1 pint/2½ cups water, the cinnamon stick, sugar and honey and bring to the boil, stirring constantly. Reduce the heat, cover and simmer very gently for 10–12 minutes, then remove the pan from the heat. Stir in the lemon juice. Allow to cool, then pour the mixture into a bowl and chill in the refrigerator for 1–2 hours before serving.

Energy 160kcal/682kJ; Protein 2.6g; Carbohydrate 38.9g, of which sugars 38.9g; Fat 0.4g, of which saturates 0g, of which polyunsaturates 0.1g; Cholesterol 0mg; Calcium 57mg; Fibre 4.8g; Sodium 10mg.

ICED CLEMENTINES ★

THESE PRETTY, SORBET-FILLED FRUITS FREEZE WELL, AND WILL PROVE PERFECT FOR AN IMPROMPTU SUMMER PARTY, A PICNIC OR SIMPLY A REFRESHING FAT-FREE TREAT ON A HOT SUMMER'S AFTERNOON.

MAKES TWELVE

INGREDIENTS
16 large clementines
175g/6oz/scant 1 cup caster (superfine) sugar
105ml/7 tbsp water
juice of 2 lemons
a little fresh orange juice (if necessary)
fresh mint or lemon balm leaves, to decorate

VARIATION
Use satsumas or mandarin oranges in place of clementines.

1 Slice the tops off 12 of the clementines to make lids. Set aside on a baking sheet. Loosen the clementine flesh with a sharp knife then carefully scoop it out into a bowl, keeping the shells intact. Scrape out and discard as much of the membrane from the shells as possible. Add the shells to the lids and put them in the freezer.

2 Put the sugar and water in a heavy pan and heat gently, stirring, until the sugar dissolves. Bring to the boil, then boil for 3 minutes without stirring. Remove the pan from the heat and leave the syrup to cool, then stir in the lemon juice.

3 Finely grate the rind from the remaining 4 clementines. Squeeze the fruits and add the juice and rind to the syrup.

4 Process the clementine flesh in a blender or food processor, then press it through a sieve (strainer) placed over a bowl to extract as much juice as possible. Add this juice to the syrup. You need about 900ml/1½ pints/3¾ cups of liquid. Make up with fresh orange juice, if necessary.

5 To make the sorbet (sherbet) by hand: Pour the mixture into a shallow freezerproof container and freeze for 3–4 hours, beating twice as the sorbet thickens. **Using an ice cream maker:** Churn the mixture until it holds its shape.

6 Pack the sorbet into the clementine shells, mounding them up slightly in the centre. Position the lids and return to the freezer for several hours or overnight.

7 Transfer the frozen clementines to the refrigerator about 30 minutes before serving, to soften. Serve decorated with mint or lemon balm leaves.

Energy 77kcal/329kJ; Protein 0.6g; Carbohydrate 19.9g, of which sugars 19.9g; Fat 0.1g, of which saturates 0g, of which polyunsaturates 0g; Cholesterol 0mg; Calcium 24mg; Fibre 0.6g; Sodium 3mg.

LEMON SORBET ★

THIS SMOOTH, TANGY SORBET ORIGINATES FROM THE ANDALUCIA REGION OF SPAIN, AND CREATES A REFRESHING LIGHT DESSERT THAT ALL THE FAMILY WILL ENJOY.

SERVES SIX

INGREDIENTS
  200g/7oz/1 cup caster
    (superfine) sugar
  300ml/½ pint/1¼ cups water
  4 lemons, washed
  1 large (US extra large) egg white
  a little granulated sugar,
    for sprinkling

1 Put the caster sugar and water into a heavy pan and bring slowly to the boil, stirring occasionally, until the sugar has just dissolved.

2 Using a vegetable peeler, pare the rind thinly from two of the lemons directly into the pan. Simmer for about 2 minutes without stirring, then remove the pan from the heat. Leave the syrup to cool, then chill.

3 Squeeze the juice from all the lemons and carefully strain it into the syrup, making sure all the pips (seeds) are removed. Take the lemon rind out of the syrup and set it aside until you make the decoration.

4 If you have an ice cream maker, strain the syrup into the machine tub and churn for 10 minutes, or until thickening.

5 In a bowl, lightly whisk the egg white with a fork, then pour it into the machine. Continue to churn for 10–15 minutes, or until firm enough to scoop.

6 If working by hand, strain the syrup into a plastic tub or a similar shallow freezerproof container and freeze for 4 hours, or until the mixture is mushy.

7 Scoop the mushy mixture into a blender or food processor and process until smooth. Whisk the egg white with a fork until it is just frothy. Spoon the sorbet back into its container; beat in the egg white. Freeze for 1 hour.

8 To make the sugared rind decoration, use the blanched rind from step 2. Cut into very thin strips and sprinkle with granulated sugar on a plate. Scoop the sorbet into bowls or glasses; decorate with the sugared lemon rind.

VARIATION
Sorbet (sherbet) can be made from any citrus fruit. As a guide, you will need 300ml/½ pint/1¼ cups of fresh fruit juice and the pared rind of half the squeezed fruits. For example, use four oranges or two oranges and two lemons, or, to make a grapefruit sorbet, use the rind of one ruby grapefruit and the juice of two.

Energy 133kcal/569kJ; Protein 0.7g; Carbohydrate 34.8g, of which sugars 34.8g; Fat 0g, of which saturates 0g, of which polyunsaturates 0g; Cholesterol 0mg; Calcium 18mg; Fibre 0g; Sodium 12mg.

WATERMELON ICE ★

THIS SIMPLE, REFRESHING FAT-FREE DESSERT IS PERFECT AFTER A HOT AND SPICY MEAL. THE AROMATIC FLAVOUR OF KAFFIR LIME LEAVES GOES PERFECTLY WELL WITH WATERMELON.

SERVES SIX

INGREDIENTS

   90ml/6 tbsp caster (superfine) sugar
   4 kaffir lime leaves, torn into
     small pieces
   500g/1¼lb watermelon

1 Put the sugar and lime leaves in a pan with 105ml/7 tbsp water. Heat gently until the sugar has dissolved, then pour into a large bowl and set aside to cool.

2 Cut the watermelon into wedges with a large knife. Cut the flesh from the rind, remove and discard the seeds and chop the flesh. Place the flesh in a blender or food processor and process to a slush, then mix in the sugar syrup. Chill for 3–4 hours.

3 Strain the chilled mixture into a shallow freezerproof container and freeze for 2 hours, then beat with a fork to break up the ice crystals. Freeze for a further 3 hours, beating at half-hourly intervals, then freeze until firm. Transfer the ice to the refrigerator about 30 minutes before serving.

Energy 85kcal/363kJ; Protein 0.5g; Carbohydrate 21.6g, of which sugars 21.6g; Fat 0.3g, of which saturates 0.1g, of which polyunsaturates 0.1g; Cholesterol 0mg; Calcium 14mg; Fibre 0.1g; Sodium 3mg.

PEACH AND ALMOND GRANITA ★★★

INFUSED ALMONDS MAKE A RICHLY FLAVOURED "MILK" THAT FORMS THE BASIS OF THIS LIGHT, TANGY DESSERT, WHICH WOULD BE THE IDEAL CHOICE TO FOLLOW A FILLING MAIN COURSE.

SERVES SIX

INGREDIENTS
115g/4oz/1 cup ground almonds
900ml/1½ pints/3¾ cups water
150g/5oz/¾ cup caster
  (superfine) sugar
5ml/1 tsp almond extract
juice of 2 lemons
6 fresh peaches
amaretto liqueur, to serve (optional)

1 Put the ground almonds in a pan and pour in 600ml/1 pint/2½ cups of the water. Bring just to the boil, then reduce the heat and simmer gently for 2 minutes. Remove from the heat and leave to stand for 30 minutes.

2 Strain the mixture through a fine sieve (strainer) placed over a bowl, and press lightly with the back of a spoon to extract as much liquid as possible. Pour the liquid into a clean, heavy pan. Discard the infused almonds.

3 Add the sugar and almond extract to the pan, with half the lemon juice and the remaining water. Heat gently until the sugar dissolves, then bring to the boil. Reduce the heat and simmer gently for 3 minutes without stirring, taking care that the almond syrup does not boil over. Leave to cool.

COOK'S TIP
If you want to make the granita ahead, use all the peach flesh in the mixture, and serve in tall glasses.

4 Cut the peaches in half and remove the stones (pits). Using a small knife, scoop out about half the flesh to enlarge the cavities. Put the flesh in a blender or food processor. Brush the exposed flesh with the remaining lemon juice; chill the peaches.

5 Add the almond syrup to the peach flesh in the blender or food processor, and process until smooth. Pour into a shallow freezerproof container and freeze until ice crystals have formed around the edges. Stir with a fork, then freeze again until more crystals have formed around the edges. Repeat until the mixture has the consistency of crushed ice.

6 Lightly break up the granita with a fork to loosen the mixture. Spoon into the peach halves and place two on each serving plate. Drizzle a little amaretto liqueur over the top, if you like.

Energy 239kcal/1005kJ; Protein 4.9g; Carbohydrate 32.8g, of which sugars 32.3g; Fat 10.8g, of which saturates 0.9g, of which polyunsaturates 2g; Cholesterol 0mg; Calcium 64mg; Fibre 2.5g; Sodium 5mg.

CLEMENTINES WITH STAR ANISE ★

THIS FRESH FAT-FREE DESSERT, DELICATELY FLAVOURED WITH MULLING SPICES, IS IDEAL FOR WARMING A WINTER'S DAY AND IT MAKES THE PERFECT ENDING FOR A LOW-FAT MEDITERRANEAN-STYLE MEAL.

SERVES SIX

INGREDIENTS
350ml/12fl oz/1½ cups sweet
   dessert wine
75g/3oz/⅓ cup caster (superfine)
   sugar
6 star anise
1 cinnamon stick
1 vanilla pod (bean)
1 strip thinly pared lime rind
30ml/2 tbsp Cointreau
12 clementines

VARIATIONS
• Tangerines or small oranges can be used instead of clementines.
• Use thinly pared lemon rind in place of lime rind.

1 Put the wine, sugar, star anise and cinnamon stick in a pan. Split the vanilla pod and add it to the pan with the lime rind. Bring to the boil, then reduce the heat and simmer for 10 minutes. Remove the pan from the heat and allow to cool, then stir in the Cointreau.

COOK'S TIPS
When buying vanilla pods (beans), test them for freshness – simply bend the vanilla pods: they should be supple and resilient. To obtain a stronger flavour from a vanilla pod (bean), use the tiny, oily seeds rather than infusing the whole pod. Cut the pod in half lengthways, and using the tip of a sharp knife, scrape out the seeds from inside the opened pod, then add the seeds directly to the dish as required.

2 Peel the clementines, removing all the pith and white membranes. Cut some of the clementines in half and arrange them all in a glass dish. Pour over the spiced wine and chill overnight.

Energy 145kcal/612kJ; Protein 0.9g; Carbohydrate 23.5g, of which sugars 23.5g; Fat 0.1g, of which saturates 0g, of which polyunsaturates 0g; Cholesterol 0mg; Calcium 40mg; Fibre 1g; Sodium 12mg.

ZABAGLIONE ★★

THIS LOW-FAT WARM EGG CUSTARD IS A MUCH-LOVED CLASSIC ITALIAN DESSERT. TRADITIONALLY MADE WITH MARSALA, YOU CAN REPLACE THIS FORTIFIED WINE WITH MADEIRA OR SWEET SHERRY.

SERVES FOUR

INGREDIENTS
4 egg yolks
50g/2oz/¼ cup caster
   (superfine) sugar
60ml/4 tbsp Marsala, Madeira or
   sweet sherry
amaretti, to serve (optional)

VARIATION
For a special treat, make a chocolate version of this low-fat dessert. Whisk in 30ml/2 tbsp unsweetened cocoa powder with the wine or sherry and serve dusted with cocoa powder and icing sugar.

1 Place the egg yolks and sugar in a large heatproof bowl, and whisk with an electric whisk until the mixture is pale and thick.

2 Gradually add the Marsala, Madeira or sherry to the egg mixture, 15ml/ 1 tbsp at a time, whisking well after each addition.

3 Place the bowl over a pan of gently simmering water and continue to whisk for 5–7 minutes, or until the mixture becomes thick; when the beaters are lifted they should leave a thick trail on the surface of the mixture. Do not be tempted to underbeat the mixture, as the zabaglione will be too runny and will be likely to separate.

4 Pour into four warmed, stemmed glasses and serve immediately with amaretti for dipping, if you like.

COOK'S TIP
Zabaglione is also delicious served as a sauce with cooked fruit. Try serving it with poached pears, grilled (broiled) peaches or baked bananas to create a really special dessert.

Energy 134kcal/561kJ; Protein 3g; Carbohydrate 14.9g, of which sugars 14.9g; Fat 5.5g, of which saturates 1.6g, of which polyunsaturates 0.6g; Cholesterol 202mg; Calcium 31mg; Fibre 0g; Sodium 10mg.

FOCACCIA ★

THIS IS A DELICIOUS FLATTISH BREAD, ORIGINATING FROM GENOA IN ITALY, MADE WITH FLOUR, OLIVE OIL AND SALT. THERE ARE MANY VARIATIONS, FROM MANY REGIONS, INCLUDING STUFFED VARIETIES AND VERSIONS TOPPED WITH ONIONS, OLIVES OR HERBS.

MAKES ONE LOAF
SERVES EIGHT

INGREDIENTS
  25g/1oz fresh yeast
  400g/14oz/3½ cups strong white
    bread flour
  10ml/2 tsp salt
  45ml/3 tbsp olive oil
  10ml/2 tsp coarse sea salt

1 Lightly grease a 25cm/10in tart tin (pan) and set aside. In a small bowl, dissolve the yeast in 120ml/4fl oz/½ cup warm water. Allow to stand for 10 minutes. Sift the flour into a large bowl, make a well in the centre, and add the yeast mixture, salt and 25ml/1½ tbsp oil. Mix in the flour and add more water, if necessary, mixing to make a dough.

2 Turn out on to a floured surface and knead the dough for about 10 minutes, or until smooth and elastic. Return to the bowl, cover with a cloth, and leave to rise in a warm place for 2–2½ hours, or until the dough has doubled in bulk.

3 Knock back (punch down) the dough and knead again for a few minutes. Press into the prepared tin, and cover with a damp cloth. Leave to rise in a warm place for 30 minutes.

4 Preheat the oven to 200°C/400°F/Gas 6. Poke the dough all over with your fingers, to make little dimples in the surface. Brush the remaining oil over the dough using a pastry brush. Sprinkle with the coarse sea salt.

5 Bake in the oven for 20–25 minutes, or until the bread is a pale golden colour. Carefully remove from the tin and leave to cool on a wire rack. The bread is best eaten on the day of making, but it also freezes very well.

Energy 208kcal/878kJ; Protein 4.7g; Carbohydrate 38.9g, of which sugars 0.8g; Fat 4.8g, of which saturates 0.7g, of which polyunsaturates 0.6g; Cholesterol 0mg; Calcium 70mg; Fibre 1.6g; Sodium 493mg.

CIABATTA ★

THIS IRREGULAR-SHAPED ITALIAN BREAD IS SO CALLED BECAUSE IT LOOKS LIKE AN OLD SHOE OR SLIPPER. IT IS MADE WITH A VERY WET DOUGH FLAVOURED WITH OLIVE OIL; COOKING PRODUCES A BREAD WITH HOLES AND A WONDERFULLY CHEWY CRUST.

MAKES THREE LOAVES
EACH LOAF SERVES FOUR

INGREDIENTS
For the biga starter
    7g/¼oz fresh yeast
    175–200ml/6–7fl oz/¾–scant 1 cup
      lukewarm water
    350g/12oz/3 cups unbleached plain
      (all-purpose) flour, plus extra for
      dusting
For the dough
    15g/½oz fresh yeast
    400ml/14fl oz/1⅔ cups lukewarm
      water
    60ml/4 tbsp lukewarm milk
    500g/1¼lb/5 cups unbleached strong
      white bread flour
    10ml/2 tsp salt
    45ml/3 tbsp extra virgin olive oil

1 In a small bowl, cream the yeast for the biga starter with a little of the water. Sift the flour into a large bowl. Gradually mix in the yeast mixture and enough of the remaining water to form a firm dough.

2 Turn out the biga starter dough on to a lightly floured surface and knead for about 5 minutes, or until smooth and elastic. Return the dough to the bowl, cover with lightly oiled clear film (plastic wrap) and leave in a warm place for 12–15 hours, or until the dough has risen and is starting to collapse.

3 Sprinkle three baking sheets with flour. In a small bowl, mix the yeast for the dough with a little of the water until creamy, then mix in the remainder. Add the yeast mixture to the biga and gradually mix in.

4 Mix in the milk, beating thoroughly with a wooden spoon. Using your hand, gradually beat in the flour, lifting the dough as you mix. Mixing the dough will take 15 minutes or more and form a very wet mix, impossible to knead on a work surface.

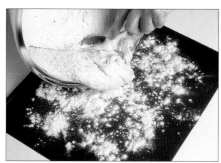

5 With a spoon, carefully tip one-third of the dough at a time on to the baking sheets without knocking back (punching down) the dough in the process.

VARIATION
To make tomato-flavoured ciabatta, add 115g/4oz/1 cup chopped, drained sun-dried tomatoes in olive oil. Add with the olive oil in step 5. Remember this will increase the fat and calorie content of the loaves.

6 Using floured hands, shape into rough oblong loaves, about 2.5cm/1in thick. Flatten slightly with splayed fingers. Sprinkle with flour; leave to rise in a warm place for 30 minutes.

7 Meanwhile, preheat the oven to 220°C/425°F/Gas 7. Bake the loaves in the oven for 25–30 minutes, or until golden brown and sounding hollow when tapped on the base. Transfer to a wire rack to cool.

Energy 269kcal/1139kJ; Protein 6.8g; Carbohydrate 55.3g, of which sugars 1.3g; Fat 3.8g, of which saturates 0.6g, of which polyunsaturates 0.7g; Cholesterol 0mg; Calcium 105mg; Fibre 2.2g; Sodium 332mg.

FRENCH BAGUETTES ★

BAGUETTES HAVE MANY USES: SPLIT HORIZONTALLY AND FILL WITH SCRAMBLED EGG, LOW-FAT CHEESES AND SALADS; SLICE DIAGONALLY AND TOAST THE SLICES TO SERVE WITH SOUP; OR SIMPLY CUT INTO CHUNKS AND SERVE ON ITS OWN. FRENCH BAGUETTES ARE BEST EATEN ON THE DAY OF BAKING.

MAKES THREE LOAVES
EACH LOAF SERVES THREE

INGREDIENTS
   500g/1¼lb/5 cups unbleached strong
     white bread flour
   115g/4oz/1 cup fine French plain
     (all-purpose) flour
   10ml/2 tsp salt
   15g/½oz fresh yeast

COOK'S TIP
Baguettes are difficult to reproduce at home as they require a very hot oven and steam. However, by using less yeast and a triple fermentation you can produce a bread with a superior taste and far better texture than mass-produced baguettes.

1 Sift the flours and salt into a large bowl. Add the yeast to 550ml/18fl oz/ 2½ cups lukewarm water in a separate bowl and stir until combined. Gradually beat in half the flour mixture to form a batter. Cover with clear film (plastic wrap) and leave for about 3 hours, or until nearly trebled in size.

2 Add the remaining flour a little at a time, beating with your hand. Turn out on to a lightly floured surface and knead for 8–10 minutes to form a moist dough. Place the dough in a lightly oiled bowl, cover with lightly oiled clear film and leave to rise, in a warm place, for about 1 hour.

3 Knock back (punch down) the dough, turn out on to a floured surface and divide into three equal pieces. Shape each into a ball and then into a 15 x 7.5cm/6 x 3in rectangle. Fold the bottom third up lengthways and the top third down and press down. Seal the edges. Repeat two or three more times until each loaf is an oblong. Leave to rest for a few minutes between foldings.

4 Stretch each piece of dough into a 35cm/14in long loaf. Pleat a floured dish towel on a baking sheet to make three moulds for the loaves. Place the loaves between the pleats, cover with lightly oiled clear film and leave to rise in a warm place for 45–60 minutes.

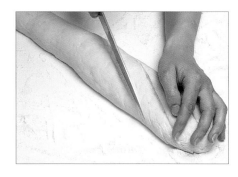

5 Preheat the oven to maximum. Roll the loaves on to a baking sheet, spaced apart. Slash the top of each diagonally several times. Place at the top of the oven, spray the inside of the oven with water and bake for 20–25 minutes. Spray the oven twice during the first 5 minutes of baking. Allow to cool.

Energy 233kcal/991kJ; Protein 6.4g; Carbohydrate 53.1g, of which sugars 1g; Fat 0.9g, of which saturates 0.1g, of which polyunsaturates 0.4g; Cholesterol 0mg; Calcium 96mg; Fibre 2.1g; Sodium 439mg.

PANINI ALL'OLIO ★

ITALIAN-STYLE DOUGH ENRICHED AND FLAVOURED WITH EXTRA VIRGIN OLIVE OIL IS VERSATILE FOR MAKING DECORATIVE LOW-FAT ROLLS. CHILDREN WILL LOVE HELPING TO MAKE AND SHAPE THESE ROLLS. THE ROLLS ARE SURE TO DISAPPEAR AS SOON AS THEY ARE COOL ENOUGH TO EAT.

MAKES SIXTEEN ROLLS

INGREDIENTS
  450g/1lb/4 cups unbleached strong
    white bread flour
  10ml/2 tsp salt
  15g/½oz fresh yeast
  60ml/4 tbsp extra virgin olive oil,
    plus a little extra for brushing

1 Lightly oil three baking sheets. Sift the flour and salt together in a large bowl and make a well in the centre. Measure 250ml/8fl oz/1 cup lukewarm water. Cream the yeast with half the water, then stir in the remainder. Add to the well with the oil and mix to a dough.

2 Turn the dough out on to a lightly floured surface and knead for 8–10 minutes, or until smooth and elastic. Place the dough in a lightly oiled bowl, cover with lightly oiled clear film (plastic wrap) and leave to rise in a warm place for about 1 hour, or until nearly doubled in bulk.

3 Turn the dough on to a lightly floured surface and knock back (punch down). Divide into 12 equal pieces and shape into rolls. To make twists, roll each piece of dough into a strip 30cm/12in long and 4cm/1½in wide. Twist each strip into a loose spiral and join the ends together to make a circle. Place on the baking sheets, spaced well apart. Lightly brush with olive oil, cover with lightly oiled clear film and leave to rise in a warm place for 20–30 minutes.

4 To make fingers, flatten each piece of dough into an oval and roll to about 23cm/9in long. Roll up from the wider end. Gently stretch the dough roll to 20–23cm/8–9in long. Cut in half. Place on the baking sheets, spaced well apart. Lightly brush the dough with olive oil, cover with lightly oiled clear film and leave to rise in a warm place for 20–30 minutes.

5 To make artichoke shapes, shape each piece of dough into a ball and space well apart on the baking sheets. Lightly brush with oil, cover with lightly oiled clear film and leave to rise in a warm place for 20–30 minutes. Using scissors, snip 5mm/¼in deep cuts in a circle on the top of each ball, then make five larger horizontal cuts around the sides.

6 Preheat the oven to 200°C/400°F/ Gas 6. Bake the rolls in the oven for 15 minutes. Transfer to a wire rack to cool.

Energy 121kcal/509kJ; Protein 2.6g; Carbohydrate 21.9g, of which sugars 0.4g; Fat 3.1g, of which saturates 0.5g, of which polyunsaturates 0.4g; Cholesterol 0mg; Calcium 39mg; Fibre 0.9g; Sodium 247mg.

PITTA BREAD ★

SOFT, SLIGHTLY BUBBLY PITTA BREAD IS A PLEASURE TO MAKE. IT CAN BE FILLED WITH SALAD, SLICED HARD-BOILED EGG OR LOW-FAT CHEESE, OR IT CAN BE TORN INTO PIECES AND DIPPED IN SAVOURY DIPS SUCH AS LOW-FAT HUMMUS OR TSATZIKI.

MAKES TWELVE

INGREDIENTS
  500g/1¼lb/5 cups strong white bread
    flour, or half white and half
    wholemeal (whole-wheat)
  12.5ml/2½ tsp easy-blend
    (rapid-rise) dried yeast
  15ml/1 tbsp salt
  15ml/1 tbsp olive oil

1 Combine the flour, yeast and salt. Combine the oil and 250ml/8fl oz/1 cup water in a bowl, then add half of the flour mixture, stirring in the same direction, until the dough is stiff. Knead in the remaining flour until smooth. Place the dough in a clean bowl, cover with a clean dish towel and leave in a warm place for 30 minutes to 2 hours.

2 Turn the dough on to a lightly floured surface and knead for 10 minutes, or until smooth. Lightly oil the bowl, place the dough in it, cover again and leave to rise in a warm place for about 1 hour, or until doubled in size.

3 Divide the dough into 12 equal pieces. With lightly floured hands, flatten each piece, then roll out into a round measuring about 20cm/8in and about 5mm–1cm/¼–½in thick. Keep the rolled breads covered while you make the remaining pittas.

4 Heat a frying pan over a medium-high heat. When hot, place one piece of flattened dough in the pan and cook for 15–20 seconds. Turn it over and cook the second side for about 1 minute.

5 When large bubbles start to form on the bread, turn it over again. It should puff up. Using a clean dish towel, gently press on the bread where the bubbles have formed. Cook for a total of 3 minutes, then remove the pitta from the pan. Repeat with the remaining dough rounds. Wrap the pitta breads in a clean dish towel, stacking them as each one is cooked. Serve the pittas hot, while they are soft and moist.

VARIATION
To bake the breads, preheat the oven to 220°C/425°F/Gas 7. Fill an unglazed or partially glazed dish with hot water and place in the bottom of the hot oven. Use either a non-stick baking sheet or a lightly oiled baking sheet and heat in the oven for a few minutes. Place two or three pieces of flattened dough on to the hot baking sheet and place in the hottest part of the oven. Bake for 2–3 minutes until puffed up. Repeat with the remaining dough.

Energy 150kcal/638kJ; Protein 3.9g; Carbohydrate 32.4g, of which sugars 0.6g; Fat 1.5g, of which saturates 0.2g, of which polyunsaturates 0.3g; Cholesterol 0mg; Calcium 58mg; Fibre 1.3g; Sodium 165mg.

RED ONION AND ROSEMARY FOCACCIA ★

FOCACCIA IS AN APPETIZING ITALIAN FLAT BREAD MADE WITH OLIVE OIL, IDEAL SERVED AS A LOW-FAT ACCOMPANIMENT TO SOUPS OR STEWS. HERE IT IS GIVEN ADDED FLAVOUR WITH RED ONION, FRESH ROSEMARY AND A SPRINKLING OF COARSE SEA SALT.

MAKES ONE LOAF
SERVES EIGHT

INGREDIENTS
350g/12oz/3 cups strong white
   bread flour
2.5ml/½ tsp salt
10ml/2 tsp easy-blend (rapid-rise)
   dried yeast
about 250ml/8fl oz/1 cup
   lukewarm water
45ml/3 tbsp olive oil
1 small red onion
leaves from 1 large fresh
   rosemary sprig
5ml/1 tsp coarse sea salt

1 Lightly grease or flour a baking sheet and set it aside. Sift the flour and salt into a large bowl. Stir in the yeast, then make a well in the centre of the dry ingredients.

2 Pour in the water and 30ml/2 tbsp of the oil. Mix well to make a dough, adding a little more water if the mixture seems too dry.

3 Turn the dough out on to a lightly floured surface and knead it for about 10 minutes, or until smooth and elastic.

4 Place the dough in a lightly oiled bowl, cover and leave to rise in a warm place for about 1 hour, or until doubled in bulk. Knock back (punch down) and knead the dough on a lightly floured surface for 2–3 minutes.

5 Preheat the oven to 220°C/425°F/ Gas 7. Roll the dough to a circle 1cm/½in thick, transfer to the baking sheet and brush with the remaining oil.

6 Halve the onion, then slice it thinly. Press the slices lightly over the dough, then sprinkle with the rosemary leaves and sea salt.

7 Using your fingertips, make deep indentations all over the surface of the dough. Cover the surface with oiled clear film (plastic wrap), then leave to rise in a warm place for 30 minutes. Remove the clear film and bake the loaf for 25–30 minutes, or until golden. Transfer to a wire rack to cool. Serve in slices or wedges.

COOK'S TIPS
• Use flavoured olive oil, such as chilli or herb oil, for extra flavour.
• Strong wholemeal (whole-wheat) bread flour or a mixture of wholemeal and white flour works well in this recipe.

Energy 189kcal/798kJ; Protein 4.2g; Carbohydrate 34.6g, of which sugars 1.1g; Fat 4.7g, of which saturates 0.7g, of which polyunsaturates 0.6g; Cholesterol 0mg; Calcium 63mg; Fibre 1.5g; Sodium 124mg.

OLIVE AND OREGANO BREAD ★

THIS DELICIOUS BREAD IS AN EXCELLENT LOW-FAT ACCOMPANIMENT TO ALL SALADS AND PASTA DISHES, AND IS PARTICULARLY GOOD SERVED WARM.

MAKES ONE LOAF
SERVES EIGHT

INGREDIENTS
  300ml/¼ pint/1¼ cups warm water
  5ml/1 tsp dried yeast
  pinch of granulated sugar
  15ml/1 tbsp olive oil
  1 onion, chopped
  450g/1lb/4 cups strong white
    bread flour
  5ml/1 tsp salt
  1.5ml/¼ tsp ground black pepper
  50g/2oz/½ cup pitted black olives,
    roughly chopped
  15ml/1 tbsp black olive paste
  15ml/1 tbsp chopped fresh oregano
  15ml/1 tbsp chopped fresh parsley

1 Lightly grease a baking sheet and set aside. Put half the warm water in a jug (cup). Sprinkle the yeast on top. Add the sugar, mix well and leave for 10 minutes.

2 Heat the olive oil in a non-stick frying pan and fry the onion until golden brown.

3 Sift the flour into a large bowl with the salt and pepper. Make a well in the centre. Add the yeast mixture, the fried onion (with the oil), the olives, olive paste, chopped herbs and remaining water. Gradually incorporate the flour and mix to form a soft dough, adding a little extra water if necessary.

4 Turn the dough on to a floured surface and knead for 5 minutes, or until smooth and elastic. Place the dough in a lightly oiled bowl, cover with a damp dish towel and leave to rise in a warm place for about 2 hours, or until doubled in bulk.

5 Turn the dough on to a floured surface and knead again for a few minutes. Shape into a 20cm/8in round and place on the prepared baking sheet. Using a sharp knife, make criss-cross cuts over the top, cover and leave in a warm place for 30 minutes, or until well risen. Meanwhile, preheat the oven to 220°C/425°F/Gas 7.

6 Dust the loaf with a little flour. Bake for 10 minutes, then reduce the oven temperature to 200°C/400°F/Gas 6. Bake for a further 20 minutes, or until the loaf sounds hollow when it is tapped underneath. Transfer to a wire rack to cool slightly before serving. Serve in slices or wedges.

Energy 215kcal/910kJ; Protein 5.6g; Carbohydrate 44.4g, of which sugars 1.4g; Fat 2.9g, of which saturates 0.4g, of which polyunsaturates 0.5g; Cholesterol 0mg; Calcium 93mg; Fibre 2.2g; Sodium 144mg.

MOROCCAN HOLIDAY BREAD ★★

THE ADDITION OF CORNMEAL AND SEEDS GIVES THIS SUPERB LOAF AN INTERESTING FLAVOUR AND TEXTURE. IT'S DELICIOUS JUST AS IT IS, OR WITH SWEET OR SAVOURY SPREADS.

MAKES ONE LOAF
SERVES SIX

INGREDIENTS
  275g/10oz/2½ cups unbleached
    strong white bread flour
  50g/2oz/½ cup cornmeal
  5ml/1 tsp salt
  20g/¾oz fresh yeast
  120ml/4fl oz/½ cup lukewarm water
  120ml/4fl oz/½ cup lukewarm
    semi-skimmed (low-fat) milk
  15ml/1 tbsp pumpkin seeds
  15ml/1 tbsp sesame seeds
  30ml/2 tbsp sunflower seeds

VARIATIONS
• Incorporate all the seeds into the dough in step 5 and leave the top of the loaf plain.
• Use sesame seeds instead of sunflower seeds for the topping.

1 Lightly grease a baking sheet and set aside. Mix the flour, cornmeal and salt in a large bowl.

2 Cream the yeast with a little of the water in a jug (cup). Stir in the remaining water and the milk. Pour into the centre of the flour and mix to form a fairly soft dough.

3 Turn out the dough on to a lightly floured surface and knead for about 5 minutes, or until smooth and elastic. Place the dough in a lightly oiled bowl, cover with lightly oiled clear film (plastic wrap) and leave in a warm place for about 1 hour, or until doubled in bulk.

4 Turn out the dough on to a lightly floured surface and knock back (punch down). Gently knead the pumpkin and sesame seeds into the dough. Shape into a round ball and flatten slightly.

5 Place on the prepared baking sheet, cover with lightly oiled clear film or slide into a large, lightly oiled plastic food bag and leave to rise in a warm place for 45 minutes, or until doubled in bulk.

6 Meanwhile, preheat the oven to 200°C/400°F/Gas 6. Brush the top of the loaf with water and sprinkle evenly with the sunflower seeds. Bake the loaf in the oven for 30–35 minutes, or until it is golden and sounds hollow when tapped on the base. Transfer the loaf to a wire rack to cool. Serve in slices.

Energy 241kcal/1017kJ; Protein 7.1g; Carbohydrate 42.7g, of which sugars 1.7g; Fat 5.6g, of which saturates 0.9g, of which polyunsaturates 2.2g; Cholesterol 1mg; Calcium 139mg; Fibre 2.2g; Sodium 339mg.

POLENTA BREAD ★★

POLENTA IS WIDELY USED IN ITALIAN COOKING. HERE IT IS COMBINED WITH PINE NUTS TO MAKE A TRULY ITALIAN BREAD WITH A FANTASTIC FLAVOUR.

MAKES ONE LOAF
SERVES EIGHT

INGREDIENTS
  50g/2oz/½ cup polenta
  300ml/½ pint/1¼ cups lukewarm
    water
  15g/½oz fresh yeast
  2.5ml/½ tsp clear honey
  225g/8oz/2 cups unbleached strong
    white bread flour
  25g/1oz/2 tbsp butter
  25g/1oz/¼ cup pine nuts
  7.5ml/1½ tsp salt
For the topping
  1 egg white
  15ml/1 tbsp water
  additional pine nuts, for sprinkling
    (optional)

1 Lightly grease a baking sheet and set aside. Mix the polenta and 250ml/8fl oz/ 1 cup of the water together in a pan and slowly bring to the boil, stirring continuously with a wooden spoon.

2 Reduce the heat and simmer, stirring occasionally, for 2–3 minutes. Remove the pan from the heat and set aside to cool for 10 minutes, or until just warm.

3 In a small bowl, mix the yeast with the remaining water and the honey until creamy. Sift 115g/4oz/1 cup of the flour into a large bowl. Gradually beat in the yeast mixture, then gradually stir in the polenta mixture to combine. Turn out on to a lightly floured surface and knead for 5 minutes, or until smooth and elastic.

4 Place the dough in a lightly oiled bowl. Cover the bowl with lightly oiled clear film (plastic wrap). Leave the dough to rise in a warm place for about 2 hours, or until it has doubled in bulk.

5 Meanwhile, melt the butter in a small pan, add the pine nuts and cook over a medium heat, stirring, until pale golden. Remove the pan from the heat and set aside to cool.

6 Add the remaining flour and the salt to the polenta dough and mix to form a soft dough. Knead in the pine nuts and melted butter. Turn out on to a lightly floured surface and knead for 5 minutes, or until the dough is smooth and elastic.

7 Place the dough in a lightly oiled bowl, cover with lightly oiled clear film and leave to rise in a warm place for 1 hour, or until doubled in bulk.

8 Knock back (punch down) the dough and turn it out on to a lightly floured surface. Cut the dough into 2 equal pieces and roll each piece into a fat sausage about 38cm/15in long. Plait (braid) together and place on the prepared baking sheet. Cover with lightly oiled clear film and leave to rise in a warm place for 45 minutes. Meanwhile, preheat the oven to 200°C/400°F/Gas 6.

9 Lightly beat the egg white with the water and brush over the loaf. Sprinkle with pine nuts, if using, and bake in the oven for 30 minutes, or until golden and sounding hollow when tapped on the base. Transfer to a wire rack to cool. Cut into slices to serve.

Energy 162kcal/682kJ; Protein 3.9g; Carbohydrate 26g, of which sugars 0.5g; Fat 5.3g, of which saturates 1.8g, of which polyunsaturates 1.5g; Cholesterol 7mg; Calcium 100mg; Fibre 1.1g; Sodium 128mg.

OLIVE BREAD ★

BLACK AND GREEN OLIVES AND GOOD QUALITY FRUITY OLIVE OIL COMBINE TO MAKE THIS STRONGLY FLAVOURED AND IRRESISTIBLE LIGHT ITALIAN BREAD.

MAKES ONE LOAF
SERVES EIGHT

INGREDIENTS
   275g/10oz/2½ cups unbleached
     strong white bread flour
   50g/2oz/½ cup strong wholemeal
     (whole-wheat) bread flour
   7g/¼oz sachet easy-blend (rapid-rise)
     dried yeast
   2.5ml/½ tsp salt
   210ml/7½fl oz/scant 1 cup
     lukewarm water
   15ml/1 tbsp extra virgin olive oil,
     plus a little extra for brushing
   115g/4oz/1 cup pitted mixed black
     and green olives, coarsely chopped

1 Lightly grease a baking sheet and set aside. Mix the flours, yeast and salt together in a large bowl and make a well in the centre.

VARIATION
Increase the proportion of wholemeal (whole-wheat) flour to make the loaf more rustic.

2 Add the water and oil to the centre of the flour and mix to form a soft dough. Knead the dough on a lightly floured surface for 8–10 minutes, or until smooth and elastic. Place the dough in a lightly oiled bowl, cover with lightly oiled clear film (plastic wrap) and leave to rise in a warm place for 1 hour, or until doubled in bulk.

3 Turn out on to a lightly floured surface and knock back (punch down) the dough. Flatten out and sprinkle with the olives. Fold up and knead the dough to distribute the olives evenly. Leave to rest for 5 minutes, then shape into an oval loaf. Place on the prepared baking sheet.

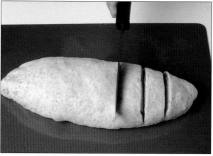

4 Make 6 deep cuts in the top of the loaf using a sharp knife and gently push the sections over slightly. Cover with lightly oiled clear film and leave to rise in a warm place for 30–45 minutes, or until doubled in bulk.

5 Meanwhile, preheat the oven to 200°C/400°F/Gas 6. Brush the bread with a little olive oil, then bake in the oven for 35 minutes, or until golden and sounding hollow when tapped underneath. Transfer to a wire rack to cool. Serve in slices.

Energy 153kcal/646kJ; Protein 3.6g; Carbohydrate 28.7g, of which sugars 0.6g; Fat 3.4g, of which saturates 0.5g, of which polyunsaturates 0.5g; Cholesterol 0mg; Calcium 60mg; Fibre 1.6g; Sodium 325mg.

PANE TOSCANO ★

THIS DELICIOUS BREAD IS MADE WITHOUT SALT AND PROBABLY ORIGINATES FROM THE DAYS WHEN SALT WAS HEAVILY TAXED. TO COMPENSATE, IT IS USUALLY SERVED WITH SALTY FOODS SUCH AS OLIVES.

MAKES ONE LOAF
SERVES EIGHT

INGREDIENTS
 550g/1¼lb/5 cups unbleached strong
  white bread flour
 350ml/12fl oz/1½ cups boiling water
 15g/½oz fresh yeast
 60ml/4 tbsp lukewarm water

1 First make the starter. Sift 175g/6oz/
1½ cups of the flour into a large bowl.
Pour over the boiling water, leave for a
couple of minutes, then mix well. Cover
the bowl with a damp dish towel and
leave for 10 hours.

2 Lightly flour a baking sheet and
set aside. In a small bowl, cream the
yeast with the lukewarm water. Stir
into the starter.

3 Gradually add the remaining flour
and mix to form a dough. Turn out on to
a lightly floured surface and knead for
5–8 minutes, or until smooth and elastic.

4 Place the dough in a lightly oiled
bowl, cover with lightly oiled clear film
(plastic wrap) and leave to rise in a
warm place for 1–1½ hours, or until
doubled in bulk.

5 Turn out the dough on to a lightly
floured surface, knock back (punch
down) and shape into a round.

COOK'S TIP

Salt controls the action of yeast in
bread so the leavening action is more
noticeable. Don't let this unsalted bread
over-rise or it may collapse.

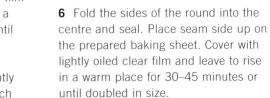

6 Fold the sides of the round into the
centre and seal. Place seam side up on
the prepared baking sheet. Cover with
lightly oiled clear film and leave to rise
in a warm place for 30–45 minutes or
until doubled in size.

7 Flatten the loaf to about half its risen
height and flip over. Cover with a large
upturned bowl and leave to rise in a
warm place for 30 minutes.

8 Meanwhile, preheat the oven to
220°C/425°F/Gas 7. Slash the top of
the loaf several times using a sharp
knife, if you like. Bake in the oven
for 30–35 minutes, or until golden.
Transfer to a wire rack to cool. Serve
in slices or wedges.

Energy 235kcal/997kJ; Protein 6.5g; Carbohydrate 53.4g, of which sugars 1g; Fat 0.9g, of which saturates 0.1g, of which polyunsaturates 0.4g; Cholesterol 0mg; Calcium 96mg; Fibre 2.1g; Sodium 2mg.

SESAME BREADSTICKS ★

HOME-MADE BREADSTICKS ARE IDEAL SERVED ON THEIR OWN, OR WITH A SELECTION OF LOW-FAT DIPS FOR A TASTY SNACK OR APPETIZER.

MAKES THIRTY

INGREDIENTS
   225g/8oz/2 cups strong white
     bread flour
   5ml/1 tsp salt
   7g/¼oz sachet easy-blend (rapid-rise)
     dried yeast
   30ml/2 tbsp sesame seeds
   30ml/2 tbsp olive oil

1 Lightly grease or flour 2 or 3 baking sheets and set aside. Preheat the oven to 230°C/450°F/Gas 8. Sift the flour into a large bowl. Stir in the salt, yeast and sesame seeds and make a well in the centre.

2 Add the olive oil to the flour mixture and enough warm water to make a firm dough. Tip out the dough on to a lightly floured surface and knead for 5–10 minutes, or until smooth and elastic.

3 Place in a lightly oiled bowl and cover with a clean dish towel. Leave to rise in a warm place for about 40 minutes, or until it has doubled in size.

4 Knock back (punch down) the dough, then knead lightly until smooth. Pull off small balls of dough, then using your hands, roll out each ball on a lightly floured surface to form a thin sausage about 25cm/10in long.

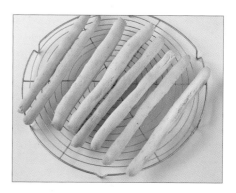

5 Place the breadsticks on the prepared baking sheets and bake in the oven for 15 minutes, or until crisp and golden. Transfer the breadsticks to a wire rack to cool, then store them in an airtight container until ready to serve.

Energy 38kcal/161kJ; Protein 0.9g; Carbohydrate 5.8g, of which sugars 0.1g; Fat 1.4g, of which saturates 0.2g, of which polyunsaturates 0.4g; Cholesterol 0mg; Calcium 17mg; Fibre 0.3g; Sodium 66mg.

INDEX